Heritage of Faithfulness
~~~
A Legacy of Love

By

Ardys Baird Soules

Waldenhoue Publishers, Inc.

Walden, Tennessee

Heritage of Faithfulness: A Legacy of Love

Copyright © 2007 Ardys Baird Soules. All rights reserved. Excerpts from *The Greatest Generation* by Tom Brokaw courtesy of Random House, Inc. Words from the song "Find Us Faithful" by Jon Mohr used by permission of Gaither Copyright Management for Jonathan Mark Music and by EMI Christian Music Group obo Birdwing Music. Cover montage by Athena Soules. Author's photo with permission of Olan Mills Studios. Type and design by Karen Stone.

Published by Waldenhouse Publishers, Inc.
100 Clegg Street, Signal Mt., Tn 37377 USA
www.waldenhouse.com 888-222-8228
Printed in the United States of America
ISBN: 978-0-9779189-8-0
Library of Congress Control Number: 2007934480

For my Children

Without whom my life would
Have been much less
Interesting, Challenging and Rewarding

Terrill Shepard
Dale Staring
Randall Stephen
Ardys Michelle
Linda Joy
Timothy Baird

Acknowledgments

For more than ten years, my family has encouraged me and gently pushed me to complete this task. I have appreciated their persistence. Certainly, without the many letters (more than 100) to Frank from my mother, and from me (far fewer) that he faithfully kept, I would not have had the invaluable material that has given me inspiration and information. Mother not only related current events when writing to Frank, but also historical facts about my family.

As I have been in the process of getting a credible story together, I have been helped by each of my children.

Randall has scanned all the photos used in this book, which I truly appreciate. He has also been my "technical support man" and I had many of my questions answered as we met weekly for breakfast. Terrill, Dale, Randall and Baird have given several suggestions about different happenings, making it more accurate. Shelley took time to read all that I had written through 1986 and helped me to make necessary additions and corrections. Linda also gave me helpful suggestions which enhanced the final story. Linda was always able to help me lock in correct dates. I am grateful for the indispensable input from each of them, making it their story as well as mine.

Helga Kidder and Judy Smith were willing to proof-read my writing in the beginning, giving valuable suggestions.

Although Frank is no longer by my side, his letters, written during our years in Brazil, have brought back memories and helped to make this more interesting. Of course, I have gone over my annual letters since 1986 which has helped to put everything into chronological order.

Karen Stone of Waldenhouse has given me invaluable advice and I am truly grateful for all she has done to guide me in this endeavor.

I feel very privileged to have my granddaughter, Athena Soules, create the design on the cover of my book.

The loving encouragement from many friends who have told me they are interested in the finished product has been an effective incentive.

Without the Lord's faithfulness all of my life, I would not have had the same story. He has been with me during the whole process.

Contents

Introduction	ix
My Childhood 1926-1938	1
Teen Years 1939-1944	9
College and Nurses Training 1943-45	13
"New Life in Christ" 1945	21
My Wedding February, 1946	29
Married life New York 1946-1948	33
Married Life Illinois 1948-1949	41
Norwich Corners, New York 1950-1951	45
Pasadena, California 1951-1954	49
Chattanooga, Tennessee 1954-1957	53
First Term - Brazil 1957-1961	59
Chattanooga 1961-1962	81
Second Term - Brazil 1962-1966	85
Chattanooga 1966-1967	105
Third Term - Brazil 1967-1969	107
Fourth Term - Brazil 1969-1973	115
Recife to Pittsfield, Massachusetts 1974	129
Grace Church Congregational 1974-1980	133
The Year of the Weddings 1981	139
Our last years in Pittsfield 1981-1984	143
International Students, Inc. 1984-1986	147
Frank's illness 1986	151
Family Reunion July, 1986	161

Part Two

International Students, Inc.	167
Travels	177
Medical Interludes	201
Family Reunion July, 2006	205

Introduction

My life has taken many different directions, with God playing a direct or indirect part throughout my 80 years. Recently, I have moved into the Caldsted Retirement Home in Chattanooga, Tennessee. It's been a long and interesting road from Pasadena, California to my present residence. I've been privileged to have visited all 50 states and to have lived in Brazil for seventeen years. Trusting God to keep me safe and to appreciate a sense of humor has helped to keep me balanced.

Music has always been a big part of my life. Two pianos were in the dining room—Mother was teaching "little fingers to count" most of her life. I sang in groups and on my own. Later, as I was raising my family, my husband's trumpet playing was the norm. Hardly a day passed without that golden tone filling the air. It seems natural to introduce my story with the words of a song. Steve Green wrote the music for the song, "Find us Faithful" in 1988. Jon Mohr wrote the words.

We're pilgrims on the journey
Of the narrow road
And those who've gone before us line the way
Cheering on the faithful, encouraging the weary
Their lives a stirring testament to God's sustaining grace

Surrounded by so great a cloud of witnesses
Let us run the race not only for the prize
But as those who've gone before us
Let us leave to those behind us
The heritage of faithfulness passed on through godly lives.

CHORUS
Oh may all who come behind us find us faithful
May the fire of our devotion light their way
May the footprints that we leave
Lead them to believe
And the lives we live inspire them to obey
Oh may all who come behind us find us faithful.

After all our hopes and dreams have come and gone
And our children sift through all we've left behind
May the clues that they discover and the memories they uncover
Become the light that leads them to the road we each must find.

Repeat Chorus
Oh may all who come behind us find us faithful
Oh may all who come behind us find us faithful.

My Childhood 1926-1939

*We're pilgrims on the journey
Of the narrow road*

My life began in Pasadena, California where I, Ardys Caroline Baird, joined my parents and eight year old sister, Janet. Mom was especially thankful to welcome a healthy 10 lb. baby, as she had experienced four miscarriages in the previous eight years. Mom and Dad were teachers: Dad teaching science in high school and Mom teaching piano at home. They had both taught school in Idaho and Los Angeles at a Free Methodist boarding school before coming to Pasadena. They were both "pilgrims" in our Christian home. However, it was not until I was 19 that I joined them on that pilgrim journey.

My parents, Merle and Earl Baird shortly after their marriage

Dad started the Photography Department in the Pasadena school system, after teaching math and science for many years. As a photography teacher, he took every opportunity to use his girls as models. My first recorded experience was when Dad hung me from a clothesline, securing me in place with a misplaced diaper. I was probably seven or eight months and judging from my smile, I was having a ball. I daresay Mom was not so happy.

"Hung out to dry"

Whooping cough threatened my life when I was only a few months old, but I completely recovered to become a happy and quite mischievous child. How thankful we are that vaccines are now available so that children no longer need to suffer from such serious diseases.

Stories that have been relayed to me tell of the time I broke the glass in our front door and inexplicably put some broken pieces in my mouth. Mom held me upside down and retrieved the "culprits," thus saving me from another crisis. When I started nursery school, I decided it was more fun to take off the piano keys from the toy piano than to play them. Later, I enjoyed playing the real thing. Returning from nursery school, I told my mother there was a funny boy in school. "I like him, but I don't love him." Another time (copied from my Baby Book) my sister scolded me for getting into her things, and I answered, "I guess I have my rights."

My Childhood 1926 -1939

There were two houses on our lot, and some of the time we lived in the rear one, a two-story bungalow. There was one occasion when Mom cautioned me to be careful as I was at the top of the stairs. "Don't fall, Ardys," and I answered back with confidence, "I won't." After a rough passage bumping down the whole way, I looked up and admitted, "But I did." Despite these antics, my childhood was fairly normal. I loved to follow Dad when he was doing odd jobs around the house. He was working with putty one day as he repaired a window. I asked him for my "buzzy." He did not make the connection and asked me what it was. In a very irritated tone, I said, "If you'll give me my buzzy, I'll show you what it is." The first time I went to Sunday school at the Tremont Baptist Church, Mother asked me what they did. I said, "They singed, and singed, and singed."

Ardy at play

My sister, Nayda, joined our family when I was three and one half years old. During this period, Mom had had two more miscarriages. My long blond curls had to be cut so Mom could spend more time with the new baby. That day, I kept looking in the mirror and laughing at my new image. I was describing my sister to a friend of Mom's saying, "She is just like a little bead—a little circle."

Ardy – dressed up

3

Once when I was in the back seat of the car while Dad was driving, I somehow opened the back door. This caught Dad's attention and he reacted immediately as he reached out for my skirt and pulled me in. Thus I avoided a calamitous fall to the pavement. My guardian Angel seemed to be watching over me. I guess I was quite independent from the start. Mom recorded that once I was told not to sing at the table, so I jumped up, stood by the chair and kept on singing.

William Shepard   Laura Shepard

Only Mom's parents were alive when I was a little girl. Grandpa Shepard, (William E.) was a Nazarene evangelist and he died when I was four years old. A lady in his church was telling my grandfather that he only dressed for looks and he replied, "My dear sister, I certainly do. If I didn't, I'd wear gunny sacks." The only thing I remember about him is that we liked to take walks together. Grandma Laura was not well most of the eight years she lived as a widow. First, she would move to an apartment, then into our home. This scenario was replayed several times with Dad moving her from one place to another. She passed away, at age 79, when I was 12.

My Childhood 1926 -1939

In a letter Mom wrote years later, she told of her mother traveling by covered wagon from Grapevine, Texas – where they lived on a plantation – to California when Laura Chivers was nine years old. Indians attacked the wagon train of about 60 wagons that preceded theirs and also the wagon train that came later, so they were thankful to have had safe travel the whole journey.

In 1930, there was a record snowstorm. Any snowstorm was a record in Pasadena. Mom said Dad rushed over to the school to retrieve his cameras. He wanted to capture the beauty of the fir trees peeking out from under their white "marshmallow" blankets. As a four-year-old, I was more interested in having fun outdoors than appreciating the picturesque scene.

I must have been a busy little seven-year-old. This marked the beginning of my enthusiasm for baking. I asked Dad to break the eggs for me, but I wanted to do the rest and surprise Mom with a cake. It was more of a surprise than I had counted on. I put it under the broiler instead of in the oven. Another fiasco was the time I was baking a cake with buttermilk. Using Dad's ulcer medicine instead made that one inedible. There were probably others, but these two stand out in my mind.

Mom would let me walk the few blocks to the store to buy small items. Once I lost my grip on the milk bottle and a piece of the broken glass cut the inside of my knee. I was given a nickel because I didn't cry when the doctor stitched me up. At about this time I had my tonsils removed. I was more upset that I couldn't swallow my favorite peach ice cream Dad made for me than about the whole operation.

I was only about eight when my older sister started dating. There's a lot of difference between eight and sixteen. I was curious to know what this "soft talk and soft lights" were all about. Once I was hiding behind the couch and another time outdoors behind a bush. This "sneaky little kid" was not appreciated or tolerated anymore by Janet and my curiosity had to be "curbed" from then on.

Heritage of Faithfulness

The Baird Girls

One of the happiest childhood memories was of our family reunions at Christmas. Dad was the oldest of six and our families always spent Christmas together. Aunt Beulah was his youngest sibling, and we all called her Bubu. She and Uncle Abe lived next door, so there was housing for those from farther away. Southern California weather usually cooperated and we ate our holiday feast in their back yard. What fun we cousins had as we opened presents and then played outdoors. My uncle John was the only one with an 8mm. movie camera, so I actually have movies of those occasions now transferred to videotape. How I loved to act up in front of a camera.

Nayda getting a ride from big sister, Ardy

We went to Oakland to visit Uncle John and Aunt Lillian in 1937, and I was able to walk on the Golden Gate Bridge the year it opened. Dad liked to take trips where he could photograph wonderful, majestic sceneries. Yosemite and Grand Canyon were my favorites. When I took one of his photos to be framed years later, the salesgirl mentioned that it looked like one by Ansel Adams. They had been contemporaries. Across the valley from Half Dome were the Bridal Veil Falls. Each night during the summer they would shove a huge bonfire over the edge and cry out, "Let the fire fall." It was so exciting to watch that spectacle. It is no longer allowed, of course. Grand Canyon was so awe-inspiring that, even as a girl, I was quite amazed at the beauty of it. It was truly a "photographer's dream."

Dad also liked to fish. Occasionally, he would drive to the coast and go Deep Sea Fishing. One time he hit the "jackpot," catching the most fish of anyone on the boat. He bartered fish all the way home, stopping at produce stands along the road. Not only did we have plenty of fish, but also an abundance of fresh vegetables and fruit that week.

Another childhood memory I have is going to Brookside Park in Pasadena to have a picnic breakfast. We would do this quite often in the summer and Dad would make pancakes. That was really special.

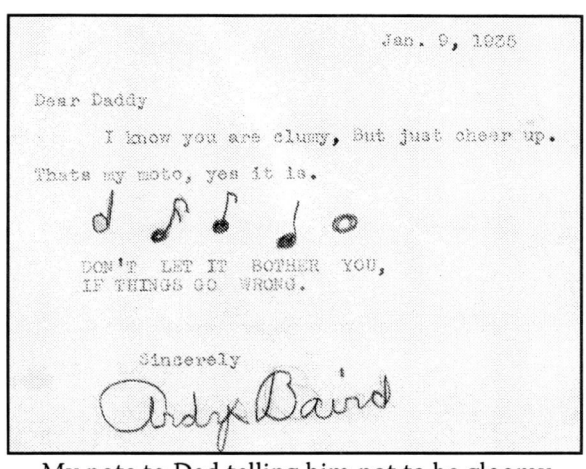

My note to Dad telling him not to be gloomy

And those who've gone before us line the way.

My parents had been brought up in rather strict denominations. Dad's father, Joel Gordon Baird, was principal of the Los Angeles Free Methodist Seminary a boarding high school. Mother's father, William E. Shepard, was an Evangelist with the Nazarene denomination that began in 1895. Before he was an evangelist, Grandpa Shepard was the first pastor in the Nazarene church in Oakland for a few months. This explains why Mom wrote about her family taking the boat several times to and from San Francisco and L. A. when she was about six years old.

By the time I was a young girl, our family had joined the Immanuel Baptist Church where I was involved in youth activities and church-sponsored summer camps. Although I was baptized at the age of 12, I don't think I had a personal relationship with Jesus Christ at that time, nor was I aware of my need of a Savior.

Teen Years 1939-1943

As I mentioned, Mom taught piano in our home, and had many pupils. Her recitals were well known in Pasadena. She was also a good cook but didn't particularly like the role. The summer I was 14, she asked if I would like to take over the task of feeding the family. I didn't have any better sense than to accept the challenge. So, the planning, shopping and cooking were my responsibility until school started in the fall. What a great preparation for marriage – I never was nervous about trying a new recipe. I still love to "read" cookbooks. Years later Mom was writing about the outcome of a pecan pie recipe she had made. She compared it to my cooking, saying I took more pains than she did. "With Ardy, it's a real pleasure, consequently it is better." I don't think that was a correct comparison, but I really do like to cook.

Between our house and Aunt Bubu's was an empty lot full of fruit trees. There were avocados, persimmons, cherries and walnuts. I think there were figs also, but all in all, we were amply supplied with fresh fruit. Dad loved to work in the garden and be involved in carpentry projects. In our back yard he had planted a wisteria vine that grew over a trellis. He also took pride in the camellias he grew. There was a small triangle-shaped fish pond by the driveway. On one occasion, a couple came to dinner and as the man stepped out of his car, he landed in the fish pond. A few weeks later, the pond had morphed into a flowerbed. A group of the teachers got together every month and they wanted to give the group a high-sounding name. As this was mainly to have conversation and refreshments, they gave it a "Greek letter" name – Eta Bita Pi.

In Jr. High, I told Mom I was disgusted with life. "The boys all act as if they are afraid of me and they call me a brain." I didn't like that at all. In those years, the Pasadena school system had several junior high schools up through the 10th grade. All graduates went to the Pasadena City College for the last two years of high school, and continued on for the first two years of college, if desired. Therefore, I was privileged to graduate with my class from 10th and 12th grades in the famous Rose Bowl. There were nearly 2000 graduates in all. The 10th grade girls wore pastel dresses and the high school graduates wore white. Those with Associate degrees wore Cap and Gowns, and the Nurses wore their Navy blue capes. The curved lines were all marked out on the field and it was quite an impressive affair.

Another plus to living in Pasadena was watching high school and college football games at the Rose Bowl. One memorable game was when Jackie Robinson made a 97-yard run scoring a touchdown for UCLA. While attending UCLA he lettered in all four major sports. He had grown up in Pasadena and graduated from Pasadena City College. (In 1947, when he was drafted by the Brooklyn Dodgers, he became famous as the man who broke the color barrier in the Major Leagues.) As I read his autobiography years later, I was saddened to become aware of racial inequalities in the 30's and 40's. He said the colored children could only use the pool on the day it was to be cleaned. I recall many happy memories of using that pool at Brookside Park, totally unaware of those rules.

My parents celebrated their Silver Anniversary on September 6, 1938. Mom had rushed to the store for some last minute purchase, and in the confusion, locked her keys in the car. She needed Dad to rescue her, but that didn't dampen the festive spirit at the party which followed. It is with fond memories that I think of my parents going on their Friday Night dates. Mom wrote about this in a letter some years later.

We usually have some sort of 'date' once a week. Dinner, seeing friends, going to a movie or musical — anything — and

Teen Years 1939-1943

Mother and Dad

we have rarely taken the girls on these. That's our time, and it's fun. I have been married 30 years and still get a thrill out of going out with Mr. B. Pretty good for an old lady, huh?

In 1939, when "Gone with the Wind" premiered, I was so excited to go with my parents to Beverly Hills to see one of the first showings. Mom loved anything associated with the South. Her grandfather, Joel Chivers, was in the Civil War in Georgia. He is buried in a Confederate Cemetery in Marietta, Georgia, having succumbed to pneumonia during the war.

My high school years were busy with my involvement in Christian Endeavor, the National Honor Society and enough dates to keep my folks a little anxious. In my junior year, a benign tumor was discovered on my right knee. This was removed, but the physician did not cauterize the bone. I was a freshman in college when the operation was repeated; this time successfully. My long-range plan was to enter the Cadet Nurse Corps, so my pre-nursing curriculum included Physics, Chemistry and

Food Sciences. It was really difficult to make up two weeks of lab courses after the second operation.

A pleasant high school memory was being in the try-outs for the Royal Court in the Tournament of Roses Parade. This was open to all the female students at Pasadena City College. It was a thrill to get as far as the final 14, but joining the seven who were not chosen to be the princesses and the queen was a bit disappointing, to say the least.

Every American was involved directly or indirectly in our participation in World War II. So many products were needed for the War effort, it made rationing necessary from 1942 on, and we were given coupons to buy gas, meat and butter. I so vividly remember buying our margarine in a solid white block. A small orange "pellet" had to be squeezed into the oleo, as it was called then, and worked until a pleasing yellow color was uniform throughout. By 1943, we were limited to three pair of shoes a year. Also, in '43, sliced bread became a thing of the past, aiming to reduce the demand for metal replacement parts used in bakeries at home. Everything was going overseas.

Wanting to do my part for the War effort, I got a summer job for the Navy at Cal Tech after I graduated from high school in 1943. I was involved with a project that measured the trajectory of torpedo heads. Caps on these torpedoes fired at regular intervals and the project personnel plotted the path to determine the most effective head shape. This was done on a "Jungle Jim" of sorts so we could actually show the path. What a difference technology has made in this generation. But I must say it was more interesting than my previous job as a salesgirl.

Cheering on the faithful, encouraging the weary, Their lives a stirring testament to God's sustaining grace.

College and Nurses Training 1943-1945

After one year in college, I entered the Good Samaritan Hospital Nursing Program in Los Angeles. In May 1944, my plans seemed to be all set to go to Chicago. Mom and Dad had lived there for five years when they got married. My cousin Lyn and I had been accepted at Wesley Memorial Hospital. It turned out they were full for the fall class and so my life took a 180-degree turn. I enrolled in the Cadet Nurse Program and I moved to LA to live on campus. Lyn entered her Nurses training at Huntington Memorial in Pasadena. Lyn and I both received partial scholarships from the California Federated Women's Clubs. No married girls were allowed in the Cadet Nurse program. At the time, this was not a problem.

People often wonder how I met Frank Edward Soules, as he was from upstate New York, and I had always lived in California. My "condensed version" is: Uncle Sam brought Frank to Pasadena, Dad brought him to dinner and it was 'love at first sight' – my mother and Frank. (It took me a little longer.)

Me in my nurse's uniform

This is a war story, a love story and one describing God's leading as He brought together two very different lives.

During the War, Dad was teaching Physics for the Army. Frank's first year of college had been with a scholarship to Eastman School of Music, in Rochester, NY, with a major in trumpet. Dad noted this Eastman seal on Frank's slide rule (before calculators) and asked him if he were a musician, mentioning his wife was a piano teacher. This led to an invitation to a Sunday meal and an afternoon of music, although two months later. Bob played the piano and I have no memory of the other four soldiers who were included. Frank's mellow trumpet was definitely the hit of the day. I guess I made a hit with him, however, and he asked me out the next week. So, just before my 18th birthday, my life made a transition from "peaceful" to "pleasantly hectic." We went to the Los Angeles Philharmonic and found out later that my folks had also gone there on their first date. He was often over to the house during the next week, and we went to the beach once with the family. Then in March, 1944, his division was shipped out to Brownsville, Texas.

Mom loved writing to Servicemen and she was an interesting writer. When Frank was no longer in California, Mom would often write him once a week, which he always answered. It seems her unspoken goal was to share with him all that was going on in our family, often signing herself as his "West Coast Mom." In one of her letters to him, she wrote, "Don't lose faith in humanity. Think of the hundred ten million people in the United States who have never played you a single nasty trick."

I also wrote Frank and sent brownies and other 'goodies' which were appreciated. There was an article in his hometown paper about his first days at Camp Bowie in Brownsville, Texas. "He was selected as a featured musician, the one man in the big camp to appear on both Protestant Easter services as a guest, first as a singer in a quartet and later as a trumpet soloist." He could have spent his army career in the band, but he chose to be just a soldier in the Infantry. He was assigned to be the driver

College and Nurses Training 1943-1945

of the Captain's jeep. After a few months the Captain was heard to remark, "I know Soules believes in God, because only a man who believes in God would drive like he does." Driving was his 2nd love next to music.

I said this year was "pleasantly hectic" because as I was writing to Frank in Texas, I was also becoming quite serious with Ed, who would soon become an officer in the Engineering Corps of the Army. "Care packages" with goodies went to both simultaneously. Mom was agonizing over my relationship with Ed, as were my Dad and my sisters. I was blind to the fact that he was not the man with whom I should plan my future.

Frank and his Jeep, Europe 1944

Let me quote from some of Mom's letters to Frank at this time. She was truly interested in the person, and wanted to learn more about him after such a short exposure.

"I would like to know more about you – your home and your family. You see, we have to get acquainted on paper. There wasn't enough time before...."

Heritage of Faithfulness

"As I understand it, you are still in the 13th Armored Division in the 16th Army Infantry Battalion. Is that right?..."

"Not that I'm prying into your private affairs, but you were so nice to open up and tell me about your girl back home. I would lose my girls right now if I tried to manage their future. I can pray, and I do, and when they wobble, I am right there with a crutch...."

"And besides the spiritual element, we liked 'you'. There is a great deal to be said for the person who is an attractive Christian. To be a comfortable Christian and not a fanatical one is the goal, or should be, of every child of God. You are going to be needed in this Army in plenty of places and they aren't all maneuvers..."

"I sympathize deeply with the boys and girls today. Their lives are so irrational and chaotic and it isn't their fault. I was such a romantic person and have had such a wonderful life. Mr. B. and I started going together when we were 17, and it wasn't long before it evolved into a more permanent commitment...."

"I upset the apple cart several times, but he was always there to right it and tie up my bruises. At 22, we were married and went to Greenville College in Illinois to finish two years work after that. What fun we did have..."

"Ardy is planning on taking her last six months training in the Army Hospital here in Pasadena. Whether she joins the Army Nurse Corps after graduation depends on a lot of things. Hope the War will be over by then and people can get back to normal living...."

"In my next letter, I'll tell you about my book. (Her book, *Yes, Doctor* was finally published in 1957.) *Until then, Adios.   Mrs. B."*

College and Nurses Training 1943-1945

Mom won first place in an article contest in the Writer's Club in 1943. It was named "Keep Singing America." Another article she wrote was called "Four Thousand Years of music in twenty minutes."

Mom told Dad once that the only thing one could put in her epitaph would be — "She raised three girls and had a lot of fun doing it." He said he thought that was enough.

She summarized my personality in the following manner. "Ardy refuses to be banged about and goes peacefully on her way. She got enough of her father's clear thinking English solidity and combined it with my Irish idea of the joy of living; consequently life to her is something wonderful and every day begins with, 'Oh, what a beautiful morning, oh, what a beautiful day. Everything's going my way.' I read once that a sense of humor lets you bend, so you won't break. Henry Ward Beecher said, 'A man without mirth is like a wagon without springs. He is jolted disagreeably by every pebble in the road.'"

My "happy-go-lucky" attitude was seriously tried when I entered Nursing School in 1944 at the Good Samaritan Hospital in Los Angeles.

Cadet Nurse Baird, 1945

I loved nursing and did well in it. I represented the Cadet Nurses on a radio program promoting the sale of war bonds on "off hours."

As far as my love life was concerned, I was very mixed up and frustrated. Ed had made it very clear that he wanted me to leave nurses training and go back East to marry him. He had just been accepted in Officer's Training School in New Jersey. This assured him of a stateside assignment for quite a while. My parents were against my quitting nurses' training and they tried, unsuccessfully, to help me see that Ed's "control" personality was not healthy. After going with Ed for two years, I was shutting out any "negatives" and seeing only the "positive."

During the four or five months before entering Good Samaritan, and afterwards, I kept writing to Frank. I would pour out my frustrations and tell him of my feelings for Ed. I said he (Frank) was the only "unprejudiced" person I could talk to. I didn't know at the time that he wasn't all that unprejudiced. He wrote me so sincerely, helping me to see the Lord's plan for my life through prayer and reading the Bible. He hinted at his feelings for me, but was always saying he wanted what was best for me.

In July 1945, I finally decided to leave my training and go to New Jersey to marry Ed. I had even made a cocktail-length wedding dress. My parents were still there for me, but they were heartbroken. Frank had been in Europe at the end of the war and his division was then sent home. When his ship docked, he called his folks first, then the Bairds in California. Let me share what he put in his journal on July 25.

"After talking with my folks, I decided to call California. About quarter to ten, their time, I got the Bairds. Whoever answered was all excited and called Mrs. Baird. I couldn't hear very well. Considerable silence on both ends. I talked to Ardy briefly and thanked her for the wonderful boxes she had sent. Then Mrs. B. came on again, and I

College and Nurses Training 1943-1945

Private Frank E. Soules

asked if Ardy had quit. She said she had come home that evening. I felt rather fuzzy, but I had to know. From what I could hear, she was going to Monmouth. (I told Mrs. B. that I cared for Ardy more than I had let on.) There was a long pause and then Ardy was on the phone again. I didn't know what to say. Before I said good-bye, I told Ardy how glad I was to hear of her looking to the Lord for guidance and spoke of how everything would work out right if we just trust Him."

Frank had a month's furlough at home before his division was being shipped to California. If the war in the Pacific had not ended when it did, his division was to have been one of many to make the land attack on Japan. As I prayed more earnestly than I had for some time, I knew I wanted to have a Christian home and bring up my children in that atmosphere. It seemed to hit a nerve with Ed when I wrote him this and he came back quite defensively. He told me that maybe he wasn't the man for me after all – that religion did not play a big part in his life. I guess we had not brought up the subject before this. After a few weeks of agonizing, crying, praying and writing, I broke my engagement and sent him his ring. He got a short leave and drove from New Jersey to California to try and get me to take him back. Although he had been adamant that we should be married right away, he countered my rejection with the possibility of our getting married after I graduated. I'm sure the Lord had finally gotten through to me, and I had peace about my decision and never looked back.

My next goal would be readmittance with my class at Good Samaritan. The director of Nurses was very understanding but my return had to be approved under the Cadet Nurse Program, as well. After their final approval, I returned to my dorm and a life I expected to be in for the next 2 ½ years.

"New Life in Christ" 1945

The first weekend he could get a pass, Frank came down to southern California to see me... Mother had been my "publicity agent" for more than a year, sharing my aspirations, and abilities, as well as a lot of family history. When he and my mother met me in the waiting room of the nurses' home, I was hardly prepared for the well-built, copper-tanned soldier whose eyes met mine with a merry twinkle. From then on, I no longer needed a "publicity agent," and mother took a back seat, cheering from the sidelines. Things were definitely different and the electricity between Frank and me would have put Ben Franklin to shame.

Every chance he got, he made the trip from Camp Cook to Pasadena and there were no "doubts" bombarding me this time. On one occasion, we went to a Special Meeting at the Church of the Open Door in Los Angeles. As the speaker explained how everyone needs to accept Christ's death on the cross to be cleansed from sin, I felt convicted that I should confess my sin, and my need of a Savior. I received God's forgiveness and I began a "new life in Christ" in August '45. The Lord has proved himself to me so many times in the years since. Frank had been 16 when he became a Christian, and as in my case, the outward changes were not as evident as the inward ones. He had always thought of me as a Christian, so my decision at this time only brought us closer. We realized we could have this unity of spirit as well as a "wellspring" of love for each other. From then on, our relationship got better and better, and we just knew we were going to get married. I'm not sure he actually asked me, but I accepted the ring that he gave me on Christmas Eve, 1945.

The happy couple

Frank had always been good in art. There are pencil drawings he did in high school when he was 16 that are quite amazing. When we got engaged, he drew some very cute cartoons to illustrate this event. I think the poems are my Mom's, but I may have written some of them.

His Division was to have been one of many to spearhead the attack on Japan. The Army reported they expected only one

Frank's cartoons celebrating our engagement.

out of ten soldiers to survive that war effort, and I am thankful that V-J Day ended and that part of the war never took place. Frank was to be discharged, and the Army rules were such that a soldier was to be discharged in the state where he enlisted, unless he had a car or was married. He had no car, but we

Heritage of Faithfulness

The following visit was made one day.
When Frankie alone came over to play,
They both loved to sing
And his trumpet did ring
Just once before he went away
no 2.

no 3 -
And then overseas, he did go
From Europe - the mail was real
slow
But Frankie did send
Perfume to a friend
and she kept it just "pretty for show."

no 4 The letters she got were not
few
But from Europe they came,
she knew -
Then there was one Postmarked "Ilion"
So his furlough, New York was the
cue.

> *Nov. 5*
> *Frank found hundreds of ways to spend a short 30 days from New York he was "took" Right near to Camp Cook and met nurse Baird in 6 days*

really wanted to be together when he left for New York to study Bible at Nyack Missionary Training Institute. I planned to attend also.

Thus, I had to go back to the Director of Nurses and explain my reasons for wanting to leave training, again. I'd gotten

New Life in Christ 1945

> Nob –
> In two months, Thanksgiving rolled round a quite different picture was found. You might even say that love held full sway although no ties had been bound.

THANKSGIVING

engaged to two men within six months. I'm sure she had her own opinion of this young girl who was tops in her class. Not very flattering, to say the least.

no 7 –
And now it is fair Christmas time.
although Ard snows nothing
of rhythme
She's sure tried her best
To give you the "jest"
Of a forecast of bells that
will chime

Our Wedding
February 1946

He was still an enlisted man, and we had to wait to set the wedding date when he could get a "long weekend pass." We had two weeks notice. I borrowed my wedding gown, and bought a veil. My older sister, Janet, used Nayda's graduation gown as Matron of Honor, before Nayda wore it, much to her chagrin. I borrowed the matching bridesmaids' dresses for my sister, Nayda, and cousins, Ruthie Champion and Lyn Davis. All the groomsmen were in uniform, both Army and Navy. We phoned people, because there was no time for written invitations. There were over 100 people who signed my guest book.

Frank came on an overnight train from northern California, and my parents and I met him in Los Angeles. That morning included breakfast, obtaining the license, and a very brief rehearsal. After lunch, I put up my hair and we were married at 4:00 p.m.

> Now- you're fastened, Frank Soules
> To the ole Ball and chain
> and nothing can tear us apart
> One can see at a glance
> That she left nothing to chance
> Cause she anchored that
> chain to my heart.

Our Wedding. From left: Lyn Davis, Ruth Champion, Nayda, Janet, Frank and me, Bob Paine, Verne Thompson, Jennings Hill, and David Cathey

The date was February 23, 1946, a very special day. My dear Aunt Sally had made satin and net muffs for us, which were adorned with camellias from my father's garden. She was responsible for decorating for the reception with more camellias.

We ordered the wedding cake from a bakery. When my father went to pick it up, it took up most of the front seat, thus causing Dad to drive in first gear across town. As a Photography teacher, he was the logical one to take the photographs, but during the actual ceremony, one of his students took over. The only element of the whole affair that did not go as planned was when we discovered our suitcase had been delivered by "friends" to the next town and ended up at a basketball game. A true friend retrieved it for us, and we spent our two-day honeymoon in a cabin in the San Bernardino Mountains. The next day we boarded a train for the north, he to the base, and I to the home of my Aunt Lillian and Uncle John Champion in Oakland. Within a month, Frank was discharged, so we came

Our Wedding February 1946

My "Going Away Suit"

back to Pasadena to pack up. We soon headed for the East Coast. My travel-filled life had just begun, and I had never been east of Arizona until that time.

Getting on that train was the beginning of an extraordinary adventure, but saying goodbye to my family and all things familiar was bittersweet. I was extremely happy to be with the man I loved and looked forward to whatever the Lord brought our way. For a girl just turned 20, the uncertainty of leaving her family was a bit overwhelming.

We had arranged to stop over in Iowa at the home of an Army buddy, Verdaine Holstein. His family had a large farm, but with none of the amenities I was accustomed to. The water came from a well and was so full of minerals I could barely drink it. Perhaps that was an underlying cause of my developing a kidney infection before I left. The kerosene lamps were quaint, and no one seemed to mind the inconvenience. Due to the lack of indoor plumbing, a large tub was provided in our room for bathing. The loving hospitality of the whole family made me feel very welcome. Verdaine had been in my home several times in Pasadena. He was impressed with my sister's name, so he gave the name, Nayda, to one of his daughters when he started his own family.

We left Iowa after six days and continued on our trip to New York State. I'm glad I was not aware of all the adjustments that would be necessary in the months to come. For a while, I felt like an intruder. After all, Frank was 18 when he left and he was his mom's boy. When he returned at 21, his affection was now shared with another. Their large farm house was a few miles from Ilion, the nearest town. Spring was still a few weeks away and the upstairs was not heated. To compensate, we would take covered hot bricks to put in the bed before we got in which did the trick. Frank had a younger brother, Paul, who lived at home. His older brother, Fred, was married and lived in New Jersey.

The twenty-third of each month, Dad Soules would bring home hand-packed ice cream to celebrate our anniversary. Frank's mom always baked something special which we all enjoyed.

Married Life in New York 1946-1948

Frank had been accepted at the Nyack Missionary Training Institute in Nyack, New York, and I had fully expected to be enrolled as well. We soon became aware that I would have my hands full awaiting our first child in December.

There was no married couples' housing available for the fall, so Frank went ahead to start classes and find us a place to live. I think I gave him a "loving ultimatum" after approximately 5 weeks, telling him I was not too fond of the "single life." And so it was that our first home was in New City, New York, in a Norwegian community. What wonderful, hospitable people. We rented one large room, a kitchen and bath from a dear couple, the Andersons.

Frank kept busy with his studies in addition to working part-time in a box factory to supplement the stipend from the government. He also made a valuable contribution to the school

Frank conducting high school orchestra

orchestra. His trumpet playing gave him recognition from the beginning. He also did some substitute directing of the Nyack orchestra, thanks to his experience at Camp-of-the-Woods. He had conducted the Ilion High School Band when he was a senior, as well. When the orchestra was invited to participate in a "Congress of Bands" in New York City, it was so exciting. Due to the conductor's illness at the last minute, Frank was asked to conduct that night. Thus, Frank Soules made his unexpected performance and only appearance at Carnegie Hall. He also played the trumpet in the 2nd half.

Before our first child was born, I got a real scare on one of the many hills in Nyack. A friend of ours was driving and his wife and I were passengers, both of us over eight months pregnant. The brakes failed and we started backing down the hill. He maneuvered the car into a tree, successfully avoiding an unscheduled dunk in the Hudson River. We were able to get out of the car, and my friend immediately called attention to the fact (ignoring her own state) saying, "She's due any day, she's due any day." Fortunately, both babies were born on schedule with no ill effects from the accident.

This was a period in history when the first of the "baby boomers" were born and I joined 8 other mothers in a hospital ward. For seven months I had been under the care of the doctor who had delivered Frank. The "old school" gave free reign to appetite. Mine was always in top shape. When I arrived in Nyack, my new obstetrician felt I had gained plenty already. Terrill Shepard (Terry) was born Dec.12, 1946, weighing 10lbs – one fourth of my weight gain. Once I had recovered from the anesthesia, my doctor came to my bed with a rather loud, unforgiving announcement: "It's a disgrace to the doctor to have a baby that big." I don't know why he took my weight gain so personally.

The night before, Frank was told I had many hours of labor ahead of me and he might as well go home. Which he did. He had the audacity to go to class the next day and take a test. Then he called the hospital to learn he was the father of a baby boy. That was the last time we let someone else tell him where he should be when I was in labor and delivery. I was in the hospital six or seven days which was customary then, so by the time the three of us came home Terry had decided (definitely not my decision) he only wanted milk from a bottle. Finding the right formula was a challenge, as was the projectile vomiting that lasted a few weeks.

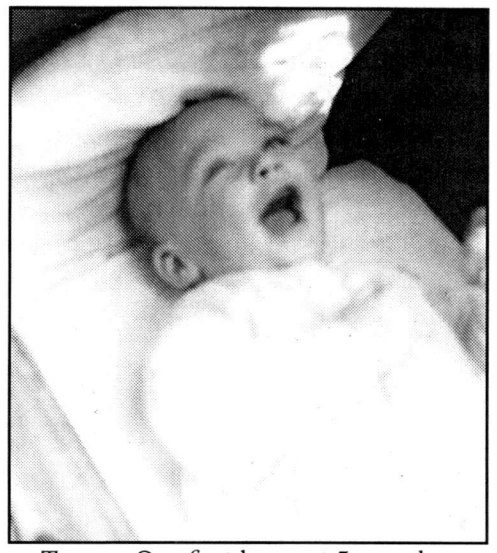

Terry – Our first born, at 5 months

Terry had strong lungs and let us know in no uncertain terms the preferred hours of his feeding times. I found the written instructions given to my mother when I was born. "Be sure to feed the baby every three hours, and wake her if she is asleep at that time." Terry was definitely in charge of his feeding times, not me.

One of those nights, when I was particularly tired, I pleaded with Frank to do the honors. These pleas went unheeded so I was in the kitchen heating a bottle when Frank walked in. I was delighted to think I might actually get to retreat early, but it was not meant to be. With the solemn words, "Don't be bitter," my dear husband went back to bed and to sleep. I felt akin to the late Ruth Graham when she was asked if she had ever considered divorce from her husband, Billy. She assured the questioner the answer was "No, never—murder, perhaps." Before many months had passed, Terry was sleeping through the night and so were we.

We were invited to Christmas dinner at Tory and Flo Lindland's. Already, we were being accepted as part of the Norwegian community by the residents. Terry, not yet two weeks old, was sleeping when we arrived so I laid him on the couch. He woke up in a hurry, however, when the son of the family sat on him. No harm was done, except to the embarrassment of the teen-ager. A lovely holiday feast was enjoyed by all on our memorable first Christmas together, and as a family of three.

After a few months in New City, we said goodbye to our dear friends in the suburbs and moved into the couples' dorm at school. I was expecting our second child in November and the apartment was rather cramped, after our previous spacious quarters. We had two rooms; a small kitchen/dining room and a bedroom. A bed and dresser barely fit and when the baby arrived, a bassinet sat on top of the dresser. Fortunately, Frank had space to study down the hall.

We had an old fashioned ice box instead of a refrigerator. I never had trouble knowing when to empty the water from the ice pan: the people living just below us would inform me of the fact when water leaked through their ceiling. We also had a window box which was a great "freezer" in the winter.

Our second baby was due a week after Frank's birthday. I felt he (I didn't know if "he" was a he or a she) was going to come early, so I invited a couple to dinner a week beforehand. I baked a cake, and we had a lovely time. A few days later, I was in the hospital again, (the nurses even recognized me) and Dale Staring was born November 5, 1947, the day before his Dad's birthday.

When the weather got warmer, one could see the four of us going to the store; two on foot, and two in the baby carriage. We filled the buggy with groceries, crowding the two babies, for the return trip up the hill. Frank completed his course in the spring of 1948, and we wanted to spend the summer with my folks in California. They had not yet seen their grandsons, now 18 months and seven months. Frank had been accepted

Married Life New York 1946-1948

Frank, Terry and Dale saying goodbye to Frank's parents, Grampa Frank and Gramma Edith Soules

for the fall semester at Wheaton College, in Wheaton, Illinois. The Army was still paying tuition and some stipend, but that didn't take care of transportation across country. [It was not until 1956 that work on the Interstate System began, thanks to the vision of President Eisenhower. It would take many years for this marvel to materialize.] The trip was hot and sometimes uncomfortable, but we were glad to be able to go. Frank did all the driving as I didn't yet have my license.

I believe we had about $35.00 to our name. We put our belongings in a luggage trailer, which we planned to drop off at Wheaton. We stopped at Frank's folks' house in upstate New York and left there with another $25.00. By the time we arrived in Illinois, our funds were getting low, and someone loaned us $100.00. There is a well-known saying in the Bible that "the love of money is the root of all evil," but we thought it would be nice to be on "speaking terms" with a little of it. At our age, we were game to try anything, and perhaps showed a lack of common sense or uncommon faith in the Lord's provision, very possibly a little of both. Terry was saying quite a few words at 18 months and could point out a bus, or truck or train, not one of which he missed in 3000 miles, it seemed.

We had reached the California border and we wanted to drive the desert at night, so we gassed up in Needles, and got the boys into their pajamas, ready to sleep. After about an hour's drive, we stopped to drink water, discovering to our severe disappointment, we had left the boys' suitcase at the gas station. The only thing to do was retrace our steps and providentially, a taxi driver had seen the suitcase and put it in his office. We were truly grateful to retrieve it and again started out west. We had no money left for a motel and by the time we were nearing our destination, Frank had been driving about 28 hours. I don't know why we didn't just stop and let him rest awhile.

We were so very thankful and happy to drive into my parents' driveway for a wonderful reunion. We had less than a dollar left, but it was enough. Our first Sunday back, we visited

Married Life New York 1946-1948

the Christian and Missionary Alliance church where Frank had attended during his year in Pasadena as a soldier. The Pyshers and the Deals were especially close friends and there were others, also, who shook hands with us after the service, giving us something to hold us over until he could find work. He soon was hired on a construction crew at the Huntington Hotel. God has never failed us in providing our every need, but many times, I must say, my faith was very weak.

That was a very special time when Mom and Dad got acquainted with their grandsons. They had a two bedroom house and one of these was Dad's study. So they willingly pitched a tent in our empty lot, fully expecting to "rough" it for a couple of months. The first night, however, a feline visitor arrived, immediately causing my Mom to move their sleeping arrangements next door to my aunt's house. This lasted until we left in the fall.

Terry and Dale, 1949

Married Life in Illinois 1948-1949

When the time arrived for our return to Wheaton, I was expecting our third child, and we felt it would be better for Dale and me to fly back east. Frank had an opportunity to drive a lady's car for her to Wheaton, and my cousin Lyn was going with them. Lyn was going to attend Wheaton to get her degree in Nursing. We had sold our old car which wasn't worth much anyway. So it was decided that Terry, now 20 months old, would go with them and stop off in Iowa at the farm where Frank and I had spent a week on our first trip east. It's hard to believe that I let this little guy go off, not knowing how long before we would be together again. He learned to speak very early and was using complete sentences by that time. He was actually with the Holsteins for seven weeks before Verdaine's brother brought him to Illinois.

By that time, I had arrived and we were settled in a two-story house in Glen Ellen, sub-letting from another couple. There was a third couple in the house also. The night Terry came home there were a number of people in the room and he immediately pointed out those he knew, and was happy to see. When he pointed at a very large man, he unceremoniously declared "fat man." He was not yet two years old and was already using descriptive words which he does to this day.

Christmas was fast approaching, and our GI checks had not arrived as yet. We had no credit cards, and had borrowed as much as we could. I had a can of Spam, which was going to be the main course on Christmas day. Shortly before classes let out for the holidays, Frank came home with a box loaded with provisions. These included a ham, many other food items and presents for the boys. They had come from an anonymous "angel" who must have been prompted by the Lord to meet a very real need. How very thankful we were for His provision, then and now.

We received regular checks after the first of the year. In his book, *The Greatest Generation*, Tom Brokaw emphasized the impact of available education through the GI Bill to thousands of veterans. "When the war was over, the men and women who had been involved ... joined in joyous and short-lived celebrations, then immediately began the task of rebuilding their lives and the world they wanted. They were mature beyond their years, tempered by what they had been through, disciplined by their military training and sacrifices. They married in record numbers and gave birth to another distinctive generation, the 'Baby Boomers'. They stayed true to their values of personal responsibility, duty, honor and faith. They became part of the greatest investment in higher education that any society ever made, a generous tribute from a grateful nation."

For me, that year and a half was probably the most difficult time of our married life. Frank was working at a grocery store and would get home about 7:00p.m. He would eat and immediately start studying. I would often be typing his papers late at night. I was emotionally challenged by our landlady. All three husbands were attending Wheaton College, but the couple we were renting from did not go into the ministry. Ministry, of any kind, demands compassion, which they both lacked. She made my life miserable as often as she could, it seemed.

I had two babies and one due in March. The washing machine, in the basement, was a plunger type with a wringer. I needed to take the wet clothes up to the first floor and hang them on a pulley line. In the winter, they would be frozen stiff before they got all the way out. They smelled nice, after blowing dry in the sun, but I didn't try to count the number of diapers I washed daily. Diaper services had not come into being in 1948, at least not to my knowledge. My days were full taking care of the family, but there was also the time spent caring for the other wife in the house, who was ill. And when our landlady would think it was time for me to clean the bathroom, she wouldn't just mention it to me, but would put the box of cleanser in the sink as a "gentle" hint. Our two bedrooms were upstairs, so there was plenty of exercise worked into my schedule.

The doctor who delivered most of the babies born to the students at Wheaton was Dr. Wyngarden. He used the Del-Nor Hospital nearly 13 miles west of the college. Shortly before I was due, Mom Soules came to help us, thankfully. Thinking I knew all the signs of beginning labor (this being no. 3), we immediately set out for St. Charles. We must have borrowed a car, because we didn't own one at the time. It was just false labor by the time we arrived, but because of the distance, we spent the night, and Randall Stephen was born the next day, March 21, 1949.

It was my doctor's 13th wedding anniversary. I had had a difficult delivery, and the doctor wanted to give me fair warning. He came into my room, saying, very forcefully, "I don't want you to have any more children for 6 years." It must have made a big impression: Six years later, we had our first girl. In August, 1949 Frank graduated With Honor, and I got my PhT (Putting Hubby Through) degree.

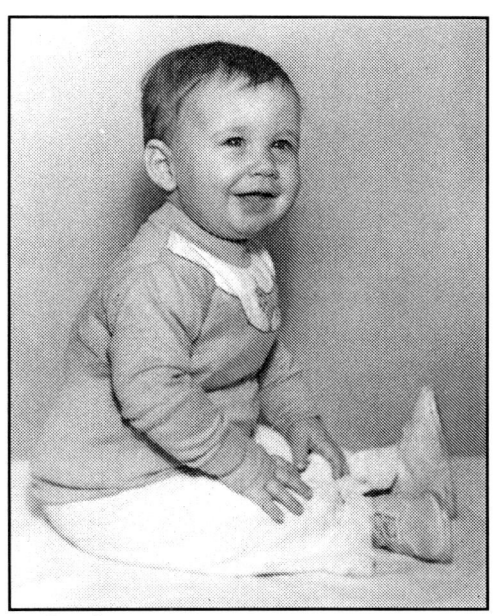

Randy

Married Life in Norwich Corners 1950-1951

We had no prospects in the job market at that point, so we moved back to Ilion, New York, near Frank's parents. He was working wherever he could, but we were praying for something that would use more of his talents and gifts.

A friend knew of his musical ability and asked if he would lead the music at a small church in the country, during a week of special meetings. He accepted and at the end of the week, he was asked to come as the minister of Norwich Corners Presbyterian Church. This was the beginning of a life-long friendship with many of these dear folks.

It was an old church, more that 200 years old. They had been without a pastor for some time. Frank was not yet ordained, so he was required by the Utica Presbytery to satisfy their requirements to be a lay Pastor. In addition to the very meager salary, we had a large manse provided. This was across the road from the church.

In the winter, there were ten foot drifts on either side of the road, something entirely foreign to me. I can remember getting the boys ready for Sunday school by "shaking" them into their snowsuits. Lacking zippers, no other word accurately describes the process. We would trudge across to the church and some dear ladies would volunteer to get them out of their outer clothing and take them to the nursery.

They were now one, two, and three. Each Sunday, Frank would start his day about 6:00 a.m. shoveling snow, starting the fire in the pot-bellied stove and preparing himself spiritually for the day. Under his leadership, Wednesday evening and Sunday evening services were started. They had never before had a Vacation Bible School, which was enthusiastically incorporated into the summer schedule. Many members accepted the Lord as their Savior during the year and a half we were with them, having come to the realization of their need of a personal relationship with Christ, not just membership in a church. It was necessary for an ordained minister to come and serve Communion and to baptize infants. This began a close relationship with Christy Wilson who would come from Schenectady occasionally for this purpose.

A large garden gave us many fruits and vegetables, with a lot of gardening that was new to me. I canned quite a bit that year, including various jams that were appreciated by all. It seems the members never tired of bringing some home-baked goods to the pastor and his family. One elder came over one day and asked if we liked beef. Our answer assured him that we did and he wanted to know if we could use a quarter of a beef. This was new terminology to me, but I knew it must be an awful lot of beef. I was thinking our little top-of-the-fridge freezer was not going to be sufficient, but we accepted thankfully. It resulted in our renting a freezer locker in Utica, some twelve miles away. Roasts, steaks, and ground meat were all neatly packaged which more than adequately met our needs. We occasionally drove into town; bringing back frozen meat, and groceries which were not available at our country store. One of these shopping trips stands out in my mind because we spent $12.00 for groceries, an enormous sum. How prices have escalated since 1950. Summer storms were vicious sometimes, and lightening blew out our water heater during one of these.

Bats belong in caves or at least near one. However, one wayward flyer found his way into our bathroom. He wanted to escape no more than I wanted him to be able to. Frank was able, with the help of a broom, to let him have his freedom. I was so relieved.

Frank supplemented his income by taking a teaching job at a local high school. They had had three teachers quit because of the challenge of a class of "students" waiting to be 16 so they could drop out. (Almost like the situation in "To Sir, With Love" with Sidney Poitier). Although he did not have New York teaching credentials, he was hired and persevered, earning respect from many of those young people. Some even decided not to drop out after they were no longer required to stay.

I have this vivid memory of really being concerned about what the ladies in the church thought of me. I was young and very insecure. Never having been a pastor's wife before, I was somewhat overwhelmed by it all. Wash day was when this was most evident. I say, "Day," because it could only be done once a week. The process was to bring the wringer washer into the kitchen along with two huge rinse tubs. Before I was through, the week's wash was ready to be hung outdoors. This was what I was concerned about. Would I have my wash out about the same time as the other women? None of them had three babies, but I seemed to think they expected this of me. This was all in my imagination, but after all these years; I still remember how it affected me then.

Pasadena, California
1951-1954

During our stay at Norwich Corners, Frank became convinced that he should continue his theological education, in order to be ordained. Fuller Theological Seminary was fairly new and he was hearing encouraging reports about the faculty and curricula. He applied and was accepted to enter in 1951.

I was especially delighted, because for three years I would be in Pasadena, and my parents would get to share in the lives of three of their grandsons. One of the elders at the church at Norwich Corners helped us to buy a new car. I had my license by then, and once again we set out for the west coast, but with Frank still doing the majority of the driving. Terry was four and a half, and as he sat with us in the front seat, he asked "Aren't you glad I can read and not bother you like the other boys?" I wouldn't say they were bothering us, but just being boys – all of them. Our trip was uneventful, thankfully, and we were so happy to arrive once again in Pasadena. Frank described the trip as 3000 miles of "boy-strous" driving. My folks had not seen Randy, our two-year-old, and they were excited to meet the little fellow in person.

Through Frank's good friends, the Deals, in the Alliance church, we were able to rent a nice house in South Pasadena, near the seminary. My sister and her family went to Lincoln Avenue Presbyterian Church and Frank was accepted to work there part time as Youth Director. The GI Bill gave him tuition and a salary for the first year, but after that, his benefits ran out. I was able to use a little of my nurses' training, and I got a job working in a near-by town for my brother-in-law, Marvin Telling, a pediatrician. The boys adjusted well in a state-run nursery school, and I started doing my part helping Frank finish his education.

I loved the work, and things were busy and fulfilling for both of us. One of the disadvantages of working for a children's doctor is that one is exposed to children's diseases. I caught the measles from one of them, but as an adult, had a much rougher time. I also contracted pneumonia as a result of this illness. Of course, I was "generous" and shared with my children. First one child, then the other two. That summer, they all had chicken pox, also, and I had hired a young gal to stay at the house while I was at work. She did a pretty good job watching the kids, but one time, she was not aware of Randy's getting into a chocolate cake in the refrigerator. He ate the whole thing. Naturally, I thought he would be sick with such excess, so I didn't really punish him. However, he came through the experience still liking chocolate, and not suffering any ill effects.

Those three years in Pasadena, living near my folks, were a wonderful experience. They got to know my boys and the boys became acquainted with their grandparents, as well as their aunts, uncles and cousins. In my Christmas letter that year I shared some sayings of the boys. After Terry got two identical presents, I asked him why he wasn't sharing with Jeff, his friend. He said, "I was going to, but I turned back my mind." Mom was feeding Dale once telling him Little Miss Muffet was hungry, and he answered, "Where's her Curd 'n' Whey?" Not to be outdone, Randy told me to quit singing, because I wasn't a radio.

Lincoln Avenue Presbyterian Church had an elementary school connected with it. When Terry went into first grade he attended there, being near Frank's office at church. Frank worked hard, doing excellent work toward his theological degree and gaining experience as a Youth Director. The last year at Fuller was extremely busy, for both of us. Frank did a lot of writing, but it did not include a thesis at this time. That would come much later when he completed the requirements for a

Pasadena, California 1951-1954

The Soules Trio: Randy, left, and Dale, right, with Terry in back

ThM. I was working full time and attempting to keep the house functioning adequately; as well as being a loving wife and a nurturing mother to three active boys. Frank graduated in May, 1954 with a BDiv, later changed to a Master's degree. Our family would soon be moving to the Southeast, which would strongly influence the direction of our lives from then on.

A few months before graduation, one of Frank's professors, Dr. Carl F. H. Henry, was the speaker at Central Presbyterian Church in Chattanooga, Tennessee. They were in need of a Minister of Education and they asked whom he would recommend for this position. Without reservation, he suggested Frank, and the session acted on this immediately. Before this, Dr. Henry had recommended that Frank go to Park Street Congregational Church in Boston as an Assistant Pastor. Frank felt his ultimate goal was to be ordained in the Presbyterian Church and be under that board on the Mission Field. As this was not going to be possible at Park St., he decided this was not where God was leading at that time.

Chattanooga
1954-1957

Frank's mother flew to California for his graduation, which was a special celebration for her, as well as all of us. Soon after, we packed up the car and the six of us set out for Chattanooga. As I look back on that trip, I don't remember much, but Mom Soules must have had her hands full, sharing the trip with three active little boys. After finally crossing hundreds of miles without incident, we drove up to Central Presbyterian Church on McCallie Avenue. Bill and Anne Allen met us and made us feel welcome in our new town from the very beginning.

Everyone welcomed us the next Sunday, and we began to experience "Southern Hospitality." One of the young men at church told his wife, "I met the new Pastor's wife – in court." Someone had run into my car the first week in Chattanooga. The Young People's group grew under Frank's leadership. He was also very active in the High School with Bible Studies and the follow-up of a Billy Graham Crusade which had been held in Chattanooga the year before. Many of these youths in the church went into full time Christian service after completing their education.

On one occasion, we accompanied a bus load of young people to Colorado to a Young Life Camp. Our boys stayed with friends in Chattanooga. Another time when we were taking the young people on an overnight camping trip, we got a call from the Allens. Randy had fallen off a slide and broken his arm. They were unable to contact us soon enough, so the necessary cast was put on without our permission. They finally reached us and put Randy on the phone. He was sitting up in bed eating ice cream when we finally talked to him. We explained to him we couldn't come home that night, and he answered, "That's OK, I've got my pajamas." Amazingly enough, none of the other children have broken a bone, but they have had a lot of close calls.

A few months after our arrival, we bought our first house. It was brand new, with three bedrooms and a garage. The boys got their first dog, also; a collie named Traveler. One evening, when we pulled out of our driveway, we noticed a candle burning in the boys' window in front of the shade. Dale had wanted to have a light on when we returned home. Had it gone unnoticed, there would have been a huge "light" to greet our return.

The boys with their dog, Traveler, and neighbor, Pat Clark.

Before we had lived in Chattanooga a year, our little "Southern Belle" was born. Ardys Michelle "Shelley" joined our family on May 11, 1955. I assume the three boys had earned the reputation of "untamed exuberance" by then, because one of the elders wrote a congratulatory letter to us saying he might have sent a sympathy card if we'd had another boy.

My dad wrote to congratulate us in one of his rare letters. He was happy we had a little girl and he was sure she would get plenty of attention from her three brothers as well as her parents.

I was interested in his reading schedule which he included in his letter. He managed to read three weekly magazines and the "National Geographic," "Reader's Digest" and "Harpers" as well as 8-10 books every month. I guess I come by my love of reading naturally. Dad succumbed to cancer in January 1956. I had taken Shelley to see my parents the month before because of Mom's heart attack. She lived another five years.

Navigating through the O'Hare airport in Chicago with a baby was a challenge. I returned home on Christmas Eve so we could be together as a family on Christmas. I'm glad my parents were able to see my little girl. In an article in the local paper, a tribute was written about Dad. Names of over 12 famous photographers were listed who had been his pupils. They wrote, "Mr. Baird was responsible for developing the program of photography instruction in our schools. The Earl G. Baird Photo Lab is named in his honor at Pasadena City College. His competence in the field was recognized by his being called to

Terry, Randy, Dale and Shelley on her first Christmas

Tribute in a Pasadena newspaper to Earl Baird, 1956.

assist in the Art Center School in Los Angeles." This was after he retired from teaching in Pasadena.

A fire did a lot of damage to Central Church in 1956, when an electrical fire started in a section being remodeled. Fortunately, it was at night, and no one was injured, but the organ fell through the floor to the basement. The extensive damage was restored and the new organ was once again used to praise the Lord. It was always a thrill to hear Frank's trumpet accompanied by Manning Sullivan on the organ. People said they could "feel" the words being played.

Those were good years, and we loved the people in our church. Everyone was so kind, and Frank had a good relationship with the pastor, Ed Gammon. I guess Frank's "neat nick" habits were obvious, because Ed gave him the nick-name "Worksheet."

Our Presbytery had meetings at Montreat in North Carolina once in a while. One particular time, Frank had concluded his responsibilities and had an extra two days' accommodation. He called me and told me to bring the family and join him. I had never driven that far by myself before, especially with three boys and a baby, but I agreed to come. Some weeks before, we had had a minor problem in a wheel which gave an awful sound, but was readily fixed. As I was driving to Montreat, the same thing happened again. I don't know what the trouble was, but I do remember the look on the face of the attendant at the gas station. I had just driven in, with a car full of kids, told him the problem, and given him the diagnosis. Unlike men in Brazil, who would never listen to a woman, (but I'm jumping ahead) he acknowledged what I told him and fixed it quickly. We continued on our way, and had a wonderful two days in the mountains.

When we had come to Central Church, it was with the understanding that Frank would work toward ordination and eventually follow the Lord's leading to the mission field. He was ordained by the Knoxville Presbytery in 1954. There were opportunities to go to Lebanon and Japan, but not until we heard the appeal for workers to come to northeast Brazil did we feel that this was to be our next home. Bill Mosely and Jule Spach, missionaries on the field, were influential in our decision.

The Mission Board of the Southern Presbyterian Church was not very familiar with the graduates from Fuller Seminary. Frank was in one of the early graduating classes. The Board suggested that he take an additional year at Columbia Theological Seminary in Decatur, Georgia. Logistically, this was a problem, to say the least. The elders agreed to cover his tuition and allow him to work at the church on the weekends. Johnny Allen (no relation to Bill Allen) was also going to Columbia on Mondays and returning to Chattanooga on Fridays and agreed to provide transportation for Frank. He roomed with a Korean student and I "roomed" with three school-age boys and a baby. With the Lord's help, we both finished that year with flying colors. He was able to complete everything but the thesis for his Master of Theology degree. Our acceptance for ministry under the board of World Missions was complete, and the six weeks orientation was scheduled at Montreat before leaving for Brazil in August, 1957.

Surrounded by so great a cloud of witnesses
Let us run the race not only for the prize
But as those who've gone before us
Let us leave to those behind us
The heritage of faithfulness passed on through
godly lives.

First Term Brazil 1957-1961

The time had come to pack our belongings in 50 gallon steel drums. This was the most efficient way to transport them to Brazil. We ended up with several barrels and a trunk. The month before, our pediatrician told us that all four children needed their tonsils removed. The boys all suffered with tonsillitis and Shelley had had a ruptured ear drum, making each child a candidate. Two of the children had the operation and two weeks later, the other two. All of them recuperated nicely and did not have these recurring infections after that.

I also needed a medical procedure to remove some warts on my right thumb. The doctor froze them, instructing me to keep my hands out of water. This was difficult during the packing days, but we had many young people who came and helped out those last weeks.

We said our good-byes to our friends in Chattanooga and started our six-week Orientation for outgoing missionaries at Montreat. We studied the Brazilian culture and attempted to get our tongues around the strange sounds (strange to us) making up the Portuguese language. Frank's trumpet was always in demand and he joined two other horn players for a wonderful trio, adding much to any worship service.

While at Montreat, I became aware that baby number five was going to be born in Brazil. Our concern was that perhaps our missionary status might change with this addition. We talked with the Chairman of the Board of World Missions and he assured us there was no problem. In fact, he and his wife had five children and thought it was wonderful news. I had

Our family on a freighter – Destination Brazil

given away all my baby clothes and other necessities before we packed, not expecting to need them again. My Mom was very helpful and sent us a large footlocker to Brazil filled with all that I would need. Of course, Brazilian stores were well supplied in this regard, but I wanted some "things" from home. It was not customary in those years to know the sex of the baby ahead of time, so we patiently waited for "her" arrival.

Our final departure from Chattanooga was from the train station of "Chattanooga Choo Choo" fame. The six of us went to New Orleans, where we visited one of our supporting churches. When we finally boarded our freighter, we were joined by five others; the DuBoses from our mission, and one other couple.

First Term Brazil 1957-1961

The 11 passengers on board: Frank, Pierre and Lois DuBose with Bo, me, the other couple holding Shelley. Dale, Randy and Terry in back.

Pierre and Lois' only child, Bo, was a two-year-old like Shelley and they made a lively pair. Our older boys, ages 8, 9, and 10, were already exploring the ship shortly after getting on board. A friend wrote me later, that she didn't have time to miss us, because all her energies were fixed on our three boys, praying they would indeed get to Brazil without mishap.

I loved traveling by ship and was never sea-sick, even though four months pregnant. We all ate at the Captain's table which made the trip even more special. Some of the time Terry practiced typing on our little portable, beginning to learn the touch system.

After nearly two weeks we sailed up the Amazon River to the port of Belém. At the mouth of the river is a huge island dividing the flow as it finally empties into the Atlantic Ocean. Marajó Island is roughly the size of Denmark, measuring about 48,000 square meters. Terry had his adrenalin pumping full strength and successfully got ahead of his brothers, being the first in the family to set foot on Brazilian soil. The city of Belem (Portuguese for Bethlehem) was full of contrasts, like the rest of the country, we were soon to discover. There was a beautiful

Opera House built when rubber was king. The more famous one was located in Manaus, however. Nearby was a thirteen story hotel – with only the first six floors occupied. Electricity was sporadic and so it could not accommodate the whole building. We enjoyed walking around the city as we were bombarded by the sounds and smells so foreign to us. It was a beginning!!

Our four kids on the playground

After unloading, our ship traveled to Recife, just south of the easternmost point of South America. The name means "reef" and the natural reef off shore makes scheduling landing times difficult. One must wait on the tides. It was a lovely sight and quite thrilling to finally land in Northeast Brazil, where we hoped to reach many people with the gospel.

Bob and Ruth Shane were the first to welcome us into their home. Their gift of hospitality was shared unsparingly with us. Their children were Johnny Joe and Ruth Ann. When Ruth called her daughter in Portuguese, it sounded like "Hootchie Anna." I wondered if she were bawling her out. Bob took us to the police station where we were fingerprinted, as was the custom for all non-Brazilian residents. The scar on my thumb resulting from where the warts had been frozen showed a reasonable facsimile of the map of Brazil. To say the least, my fingerprints were unique in more ways than one.

The Agnes Erskine School was run by the mission at that time and our large items were stored in the school's storeroom.

First Term Brazil 1957-1961

Then, it was on to Campinas, Saõ Paulo by air, where we would spend the next eleven months in the School of Language and Orientation. There was a "row" where missionaries were usually housed but our family rented a larger house quite near the school. I stayed with Shelley in the morning and Frank traded off in the afternoon, as we made a valiant effort to get our tongues to make the sounds and accents of this new language.

As I wrote to our friends in November of 1957, "We are getting used to our new surroundings, and hearing the sounds of chickens, pet birds, watch dogs and Brazilian family 'chatter' over the wall. Our boys are 'ice breakers' with the Brazilian neighbor boys and are enjoying the American School of Campinas."

By February, we had experienced our first Christmas in Brazil (in summertime) and seen the country go crazy during Carnival (Mardi Gras). Everything pretty much comes to a halt except the bands and the dancers. They are going strong day and night. I was awaiting, with anticipation, our baby's arrival, and on Feb. 27, 1958 Linda Joy was born, a healthy little girl weighing almost 9 lbs.

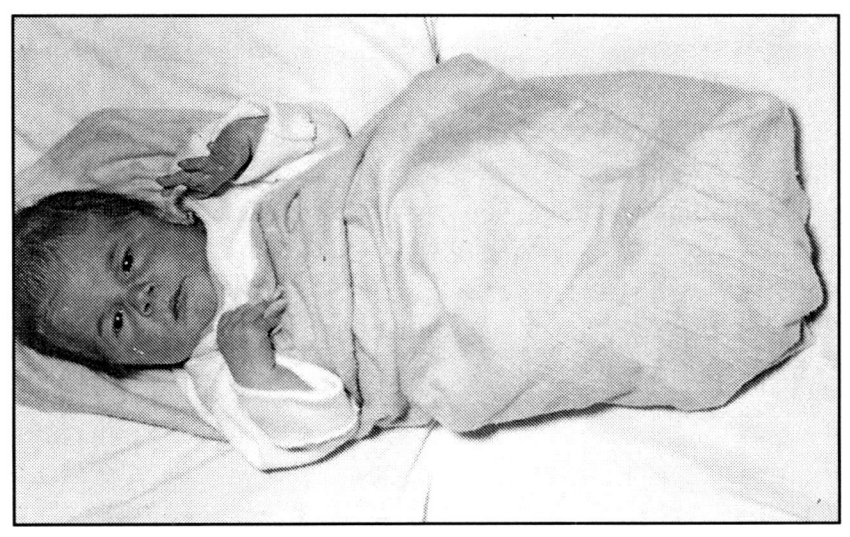

Newborn Linda – our Brazilian

I had been carefully monitored for the Rh factor, as I had been with the others, with no adverse reaction. When they brought her to my room, she was tightly wrapped with only her tiny red face showing. This was the custom, but I soon freed her from her cocoon, and checked her little hands and feet – all perfect. We named her Linda Joy, first because Linda means "Beautiful" and incidentally, because it could easily be pronounced in Portuguese. The boys' names came out with strange sounds in this adopted language. And she was certainly a joy from the beginning. In a letter I wrote home on March 2, I said, "She has no language barrier – the nurses understand her as well as they do the nearly 50 in the Nursery." Shelley had reminded us for a month, "Our baby is coming," and she was delighted with Linda's arrival.

Portuguese is an interesting language—and tantalizing in its difficulty. We were so thankful for the School of Portuguese and Orientation. Directors Milton and Carrie Daugherty were able directors and the students came from many Protestant Missions.

Frank and Pierre, our shipmate, played their trumpets at a monthly youth rally. Many young Brazilians made decisions to step out for Christ during these rallies. In small ways we began sharing our faith with those around us. A neighbor boy went to Sunday school with the boys and our maid heard the Bible each day in our family devotions.

Our opportunities were limited in the beginning due to our language ability, or lack of it. The similarity of sounds often put one in hilarious situations. One time Frank was shopping for vegetables and asked for a kilo of carrots, or thought he had. *Cenoura* would have been correct; "*Senhora*" (the word for woman) is what he used. However, the sales people were used to this type of mix-up by students from the school. Getting used to the metric system was another challenge, which eventually became second nature to us. I always liked the fact that my weight was a lower number in kilos than in pounds.

In May we began our last semester. Getting the grammar and vocabulary were the most difficult, but the fairly consistent rules of pronunciation made sounding out the words more workable. It seems having an ear for music gave us an advantage, and Frank and I were making slow, but steady progress. However, we knew the transition to the northeast, to Crato, Ceará, would present many new challenges—somewhat like a person moving from Boston to Alabama. Even our teachers thought this area was far removed from their experience.

With graduation from the Language School behind us, we prepared to travel north – well over a thousand miles. We had met some friends at school who were already working in Minas Gerais, in the center of the country. We planned to fly to Belo Horizonte and spend a few days with the Reids. I remember quite vividly our arrival at the airport; an entourage of a family of seven, many suitcases and a few boxes. The transportation from the airport was by no means up to date, and the taxi driver had to tie some of our luggage to the overloaded trunk.

As we "unfolded" ourselves in front of the Normandy Hotel, I felt like crawling under the rug. Luggage for their regular clientele did not include cardboard boxes, I'm sure. We had two lovely rooms, however, with balconies, where we had delightful breakfasts; delicious "café com leite" and an abundance of fruit. We traveled by car to the Reids' station and saw and appreciated the work they were doing. Following our visit, we flew to Juazeiro do Norte, the neighboring town to Crato. This was 400 miles south of the capital city of Fortaleza, Ceará. Crato would be the place of our ministry for the next eight years. The family was excited as we flew to this new town where we were to make our home.

The mission had rented a large house with a lovely porch on three sides. There were vibrant bougainvillea bushes in the front yard. In those days, a rent of 4 Cruzeiros was quite high. Nowadays, as the result of many years of inflation, the same amount would hardly buy a candy bar. We were able to hire

Dale and Randy with a Willys Jeep is front of our first house in Crato.

some painters and plumbers and begin the task of settling in. Our large items which had been stored at the Agnes Erskine School came by truck from Recife. Travel, which later would take only 11 hours, in 1958 required nearly 22 hours over mostly dirt roads.

Everything was coming together and we began to make this new land our "home." Crato was a very important center with most of the money coming from sugar. Products and produce were bought and sold by people who traveled from the five surrounding states. As in most of Brazil, there was the wealthy segment of the population with nice homes and the very poor who had minimal housing, with very few in between.

A Brazilian Presbyterian minister first preached the gospel in Crato in 1929, with 50 soldiers to protect him from the fanatical religious people who resented any intrusion from the "heretical" Protestants. They were content to center their lives in the Roman Catholic Church, being sure to record weddings, births, and deaths, but sensing no need for spiritual growth or regular attendance.

Four years before our arrival, a Brazilian Presbyterian pastor had begun a ministry in Crato, so there was a nucleus of friends to greet our family. I had the distinction of being the first woman driver in this small interior town. Little boys would point and stare at such a strange phenomenon. I would soon be joined by Laura Williams, who with her husband, Don, and their four children moved to Crato to enlarge our evangelistic team. Before our family moved on to Recife, eight years later, even the nuns were driving. Coincidently, 1958 was the first year that Brazil manufactured automobiles. Most of the cars in Crato at this time were Jeeps. There was one Chevy and they called it the "Cadillac."

Escola Prof. Natanael Cortez

Next, the mission sent Mary Garland Taylor who would function as a Director of Christian Education. There was a need for a Primary School and soon after our arrival some property was acquired for this purpose. Frank was instrumental in getting Mission funds for this and to supervise the building. It was named the Prof. Natanael Cortez School, honoring a leading elder in Fortaleza. Mary Garland would train many of the teachers who would teach in this little school, as well as in preaching points in the interior.

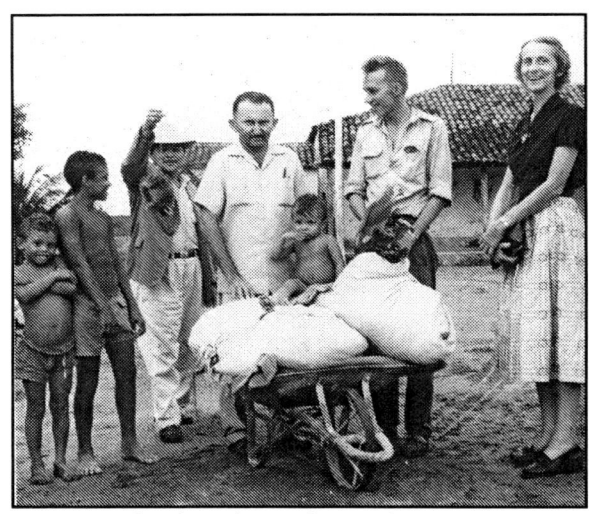

She also had the gift of hospitality and there was always a welcome plate of cookies or cake when anyone stopped by for an hour or a day. Seeing the need for more teachers, the Mission sent Fern Snyder to work with Mary Garland. She was a dedicated young woman and a lovely person who made a difference in the lives of many Brazilian women.

Mary Garland Taylor with Brazilians

Typical of many buildings built adjacent to one another, our little church had a door and two windows open to the sidewalk and a door at the rear opening onto a patio. I participated in the services by playing the little pump organ. One hot day, as I was playing, a moth found his way into my blouse. He tried desperately to get out, and I tried desperately to finish the hymn in a hurry. I finally escaped to the patio and gave him his freedom.

Our first Christmas in Crato was full of differences from the celebrations we were familiar with. We tried to keep a few family traditions alive, such as hanging the stockings for Christmas morning and being able to open one present on Christmas Eve. We added a few, of course, because the big celebration for the Brazilians is on Christmas Eve, so there was a service at church. Being a few hundred miles south of the equator and Christmas coming in mid-summer; the heat was often quite

Igreja Presbiterina. Mary Garland 2nd from left; Josafá., who worked with Frank, in white suit.

oppressive. We had our Christmas dinner on the Big Day, even though the Brazilians usually ate their feast at Midnight. Baking pies when the temperature was in the 90's made it tough, but the result was appreciated by all.

The Christmas program told the same story as we had at home, but putting it together showed a great deal of ingenuity. Costumes were made of paper, glue and hand-sewn cloth, combined with patience and love. They put on a little play and an electrician in the congregation fixed an illuminated star which was pulled invisibly by wires across the ceiling. There were many standing outside on the sidewalk. Some were just passing by and were attracted to the music and the little play. Those who wanted to interfere with this "heretical" message laughed and talked and prevented others from listening. Funds from the mission provided a PA system, and so this wonderful message of hope was heard by those who had the will to hear.

I was privileged to have a Christmas party in our home and there were about 35 present without feeling too crowded. The children were skeptical about popcorn balls, but after a first try, they agreed they were "good too much" or "*bom demais*" as they say in Portuguese. The kindergarten Sunday school used Christmas cards sent from the States to make little framed pictures with memory verses on them for gifts. To show how highly they were regarded, one little boy wrapped his in a lace doily to keep from getting it dirty.

There seemed to be a lack of commitment among the young people, who often hesitated to make a decision to follow Christ. They were active in the church, participating in the activities, but like so many in our own country, they didn't make that final step of seeing their need of a Savior.

Dale and Randy were studying in Crato with Ella Koroch, who was sent by our Mission as a teacher of missionary children. This was a tremendous help to us and to the Williams. Shelley attended the Natanael Cortez Brazilian School. I had forgotten that often she walked a few blocks alone to the school. Once she had to scramble out of the way of the cows progressing up the road to be slaughtered. There was virtually no four-wheeled traffic, but occasionally there was the "four-hoofed" kind.

The primary schools, started in Crato and in the interior through Mary Garland's direction, were important in combating the dreadful ignorance in this region. There were several professions of faith as new believers came to know the truths of the Bible.

Terry reminded me recently that Prof. Natanael Cortez had sent him a horse from Fortaleza, 400 miles to the north, on the train. He went to the train station in Crato, inquiring if a horse had arrived for him. The answer was "Yes," so he took the reins and either walked it or rode it home. He named it Pimenta – Hot Pepper. Red tape was very prevalent in government circles, but in transporting animals non-existent.

The boys loved riding their horses. Dale had a horse named "Dynamite" which he said was "uncontrollable." Dale took a particularly hard fall when he fell over the head of his horse, landing on his chin. This necessitated stitches, but didn't seem to slow down his enthusiasm. Randall had a horse named "Melado" and also a donkey he bought from a man for a paltry sum. It wasn't worth more than he paid for it. Gordon Williams, Dale and Randall "would go cavaliering around, up into the cane fazendas, swimming in the giant cubed irrigation valve," according to Dale's memory of those days. The empty lot next door made a perfect corral for these animals.

Along with their Brazilian friends, the boys twirled tops and hoops, and became quite expert at it. They even tried eating fried grasshoppers, which they said were good. I took their word for it.

There were some medical crises that first year in Crato and I spent many hours as a nurse maid. The whole family contracted conjunctivitis at one time or another, due to the prevalence of tiny gnats which would get in our eyes.

When Randy was 10 years old, he and his brothers were doing some kind of experiment with an alcohol burner. This was outdoors on a concrete table top. As the blue flame was nearly invisible, more alcohol was added resulting in an explosion burning Randy from his face to his waist. He was in excruciating pain and for two weeks only drank nourishment through a straw. A mosquito net was strung over a frame because anything touching him was intolerable. As he healed from the burn, he broke out in secondary infections over his whole body. These had to be dressed daily and he would walk the few blocks to the hospital to have it done. Thankfully, there were no scars on his face and only a slight scar on his neck. What a blessing that his eyesight was not affected.

No child looks forward to getting a shot, but some will take drastic measures to avoid them. Randy was one of those. He decided on a plan to avoid the Gamma Globulin that was occasionally given to boost our immunity. One day he locked himself in the pantry, taking the key with him, thinking he had solved the immediate problem. He didn't figure on his older brother finding a skeleton key. Dale used this to push out the key from the outside, thus unlocking the door. Dale wasn't about to have Randy avoid the shot if he, Dale, had to get his. The whole family eventually got hepatitis, but perhaps the shots made it less severe.

In February 1959, shortly before Linda's first birthday, she became extremely ill. Quoting from Frank's missionary letter, he wrote, "Just this week we had a wonderful example of the power of prayer. Our baby, nearly a year old, was sick with inflamed throat, diarrhea, and vomiting. On the 17th, she was so dehydrated that she appeared almost lifeless. A young Brazilian doctor carefully looked after her, and a nurse came daily and gave subcutaneous injections of saline solution. On the 18th she was slightly better, but if she did not pick up more quickly that day, we decided to take her to Recife where there were better medical facilities. However, rain had closed the airfield to commercial planes, our only way to get her to the capital city. Bill Mosely was visiting us and he went to the church prayer meeting that night, while I stayed with Ardy and the baby. Bill and the pastor led our believers in earnest prayer for Linda. The next morning she was a different girl – standing up, smiling and playing a little. The pastor came and on his knees thanked God with us."

What I remember so vividly is keeping vigil over my little one who hardly moved for three days. When she had revived a little, we flew to Recife where culture exams revealed she was allergic to wheat. She apparently outgrew this allergy, and within two years she was able to tolerate any food containing wheat. I am so very thankful for her and for her life over the ensuing years.

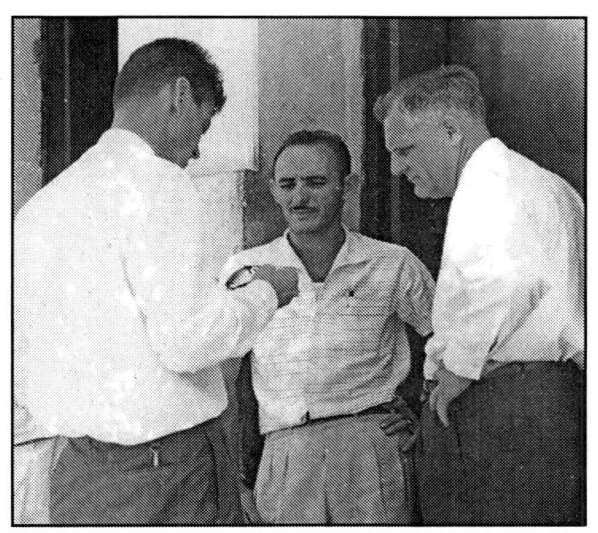

I had a young girl who helped me with the younger children occasionally. One time, I asked the maid to be sure and watch Shelley while I was gone. Upon my return, I didn't see Shelley and asked her about it. She answered nonchalantly, "I watched her. She went around the corner." Shelley had found her way, at three, to Fern's house, more than a block away.

Colleagues Don Williams and Bill Mosley with Josafá in center

Sometime during our first term I began suffering from severely swollen ankles upon waking. Soaking my feet in warm water each morning helped me be able to walk. I went to Recife to be diagnosed, and was told I had Rheumatoid Arthritis. Medical treatment was begun which helped with the pain. For a year, I returned to Recife every two months and the subsequent doses of medication were reduced. Unfortunately, I do not remember what medicine was used. I was released from further medical supervision after twelve months and was considered cured. As I learned more about this disease in later years, I realize how very fortunate I am to have suffered no ill effects from such a serious illness.

Frank would often take teams from the church to outlying communities for outdoor preaching and music. There would always be a group of believers eager to hear the Word but also organized groups dead set on disrupting the little service. One time a very vocal group called "Sons of Mary" would not let them set up the loudspeaker. One man tore apart the amplifier, and snatched the Pastor's Bible and ripped it to pieces. Frank had quickly put his trumpet into the case, but this was thrown violently into the street. The case came open and the trumpet was dented, but he retrieved it. Mary Garland was pushed rudely aside, and Dale received blows as he was trying to protect the amplifier.

Frank learned later that this group had come from the neighboring town of Juazeiro, which was more fanatic in their anti-Protestant demonstrations. The leader of that group was brought before the county sheriff in Juazeiro, who told him the law would not stand for this behavior. He then guaranteed that Frank and his team could continue their bi-weekly meetings in Palmeirinha.

Typically, Easter was celebrated by parading Mary through the streets and having a clownish "Festival of Judas" leaving Jesus in the tomb. The True message of the Resurrection was never taught in the traditional churches in those days. Three young men from our church returned to their homes in the interior after making decisions for Christ, taking their newly-acquired Bibles with them. Two of their families showed their anti-Protestant

Easter with both my girls, 1959 in Crato

feelings; one by burning the Bible and the other family by simply tearing it to bits.

In Brazil there were many extra chores to be done in a household, like boiling and filtering water, cutting and packaging all our fresh meat, and treating our fresh produce making it safe to eat. It was necessary for us to hire help. For most of our time in Crato, Anunciada worked for us. This was not always without conflict. When she first came, she had never worked for an American before. I tried to instill in her some basic health habits. We only had cold running water, and I felt that at least rinsing the dishes should be done with heated water from the teakettle. After a few weeks, Anunciada was doing the dishes the prescribed way, and I praised her. In the evening, she was back to washing and rinsing under the cold water faucet. I questioned her, and she replied with amazement, "At night too?"

She was a good cook and wonderful with the children, however, and they loved her. Linda wrote about Anunciada and her daughter many years later when she was remembering her childhood in Brazil. She played with Anunciada's daughter and granddaughter. All the children liked playing with our little dachshund, Alpha, and later on, we kept one puppy from each of her next two litters. Frank named them Beta and Omega. I guess he wanted to begin the children's education in the Greek language. Terry actually majored in Greek and Latin in college.

We also hired a young man who helped in the yard one or two days a week. One morning a termite nest had materialized overnight on the door jamb in the kitchen. Frank was going on a trip that day, so he asked José to take out the nest and burn it. José heard the part about burning it, but failed to remove it from the kitchen first! He didn't need to understand English to know how upset I was. I left in a hurry to share my misery with Fern Snyder. When I returned after an hour or so, José had repaired the damage and whitewashed the blackened wall.

Every morning the "milk-man" would bring the milk in large cans on the back of his donkey. One of my boys would take our containers to receive the number of quarts we wanted. It was necessary to bring the raw milk to a boil and cool it. After several years, we were able to buy pasteurized milk in plastic sacks. Cardboard containers were still in the future. A colleague of ours in another town suspected their milk was being watered down. This was confirmed when a minnow was found swimming in the milk!

As our first house in Crato was surrounded on three sides by a covered porch, there was a door on the far side which we didn't use. However, someone used it once when we were away; breaking in and stealing the Christmas presents we had bought for the children. We had taken advantage of our July Mission meeting in Recife to go shopping. Thus, our purchases were stashed away for some time. The discovery of this theft was a great disappointment to the whole family.

The house had a tile roof, but no inside ceiling other than the tile. Mosquitoes were especially vicious, so our beds were draped with mosquito netting. One memorable evening a good-sized rat was seen climbing up the netting. Frank was to leave the next day on a trip, and I was not about to share my bed with a rodent. My resourceful husband got out his .22 rifle, which he used on the back roads to kill hawks, and fatally shot the critter. The only downside was the hole the bullet put through the tile. This was remedied by Randy climbing on the roof and plugging the hole with bubble gum, which Shelley tells me she willingly chewed for him.

Electricity was almost non-existent in those early years. We used a kerosene refrigerator and kerosene lamps. In order to use some electrical equipment, we plugged in a transformer to bring up the voltage to the desired 110v. But this voltage was subject to power surges. Many times we would race to unplug the transformer when the dial showed nearly 300v. Looking back, it's hard to believe we had no phone for our first term.

When phone service began, we were only able to call as far as the next town. Satellites soon made phone service more extensive and enjoyable. In those days, one had to buy the phone outright, which was quite expensive. During our first term, our only contact with our families in the U.S. was by way of Ham Radio. The boys were so accustomed to hearing, "Roger, over," that they made their own interpretation, by playing games, saying, "Roger, you can come over."

Terry was studying at Ceres, the Mission school in Goiás. The whole school was able to go to Brasília for the inauguration of the new capital on April 21, 1960. Terry told about President Eisenhower arriving for the ceremonies. The authorities rolled out the red carpet, but when it got up to the steps of the plane, it was still a big roll. I believe it to be true that they just cut the carpet and let the President walk down the steps without difficulty.

It must have been a thrill for the students, along with throngs of people to witness the beginning of this new capital. It was hoped that it would open up the interior, and roads would be built in all directions. This eventually happened and the population is nearly 2,000,000 at present. Lucio Costa, a Brazilian architect and urban planner designed the master plan of the city. The center of the city, flanked on both sides by Ministry buildings was called the *"Plano Piloto"* and resembled a plane with swept back wings.

When I was flying from Miami to Rio one time, a flight attendant called my attention to the inspiring scene below. From my vantage point of 35,000 ft., a huge "plane" was visible on the ground, looking like it was ready for take-off. Oscar Niemeyer designed the government buildings. At the time, Niemeyer invited a young architect to work with him and Lucio Costa. His name was Jõao Filgueiras Lima, known by everyone as Lelé. He would become a prominent designer of hospitals and government buildings, totaling more than 70 projects in Brazil. He was born in Rio in 1932, but moved to Salvador, Bahia later in life. Lelé started having English conversation classes with Linda a few years ago and still does so today.

Typical house in the interior

In March, 1960, there was a devastating flood in the northeast, affecting the town of Orós worse that Crato. Frank and Mary Garland went with a relief caravan to help flood victims about 100 miles away, delivering food, blankets, hammocks and canvas shelters. By December that year, the new dam was rebuilt and inaugurated. Frank attended the ceremony with some friends from Crato.

As a result of the heavy rains, a trip of 100 miles to Salgueiro in the next state south took nine hours. It was memorable, not only for the length of the trip, but also for some dangerous incidents. Our way was blocked over a dam by large trucks that were stuck up to their axels in mud. Don Williams took some of his family in his Jeep (Rural) and we had our Jeep full. Randy recalls that the two men decided to drive on the side of the dam, past the trucks. He said the Jeeps were driving at such an angle, he feared they would fall

Our "Rural" managed to keep upright, though this truck tipped on its side.

down the side. And this was my "fearless" kid. But we did finally arrive at the new church where Don was ministering, and we held a special meeting, resulting in 23 decisions for Christ.

Xique-Xique was a poor community with a church and a few farms. Teachers, trained by Mary Garland, were provided for this village. Water, a necessity, was obtained by walking an hour and a half with containers on the heads of the women or on the backs of animals. To help alleviate this difficulty, an earthen dam was built by wheelbarrow and donkey power with funds paid for by friends in the states. When completed, it meant the local people could obtain water in close proximity to their homes. When the infrequent rains came, a dam was able to catch the life-giving water and diminish much suffering. People are more receptive to hear about The Living Water Christ gives for eternal life when their natural thirst is quenched.

Earthen dam in the interior

On one occasion, several missionaries were coming to Crato for a meeting. It was my job and privilege to cook for them. Ordinarily, I would have been delighted. It so happened that a barge bringing bottled gas from the south to the northeast had broken down that week. There was NO gas to be had in Crato. Thus, for the three days I had guests, Anunciada and I did what cooking we could on kerosene burners on the cement table on the porch. No one went hungry, but I was sorry I couldn't bake them a cake.

That summer, I took Terry to California where he would begin high school. My sister, Nayda, and her husband, Beecher Wallace, graciously opened their home and their hearts to have Terry stay with them and their three children. We felt that he needed this firm beginning to his high school education, but it was hard to have him so far away. Not only did he get to know his cousins and his aunt and uncle, but he told me later he especially enjoyed his weekly visits with my mother.

Our family flew to Recife and then traveled by bus to see in the new year of 1961 with members of the North Brazil Presbyterian Mission in Garanhuns. That was the location of the Quinze de Novembro School, where many of our colleagues taught. It was much cooler than Crato because of the higher altitude and a nice relief from the summer heat.

As we prepared to leave in June on our first furlough in the U. S. we were overjoyed that a recent seminary graduate, Edijece Martins, was coming to be the new pastor of the Crato church.

My mother passed away just before Mother's Day, 1961, and I was sorry I was not able to be with her at the last. It was a comfort that I had had the month-long visit the year before, when Terry and I went to California. She was aware that our next baby would be born in Chattanooga, even though she never got to see the little one. Instead of flying out of Juazeiro airport, we used the Crato airstrip on the Serra or plateau. The plane was delayed several hours; first three, then six, and finally 18 hours. Frank apparently needed all this extra time, because he was occupied overnight doing the "last minute" things in his study. When we finally arrived at the airstrip, we still had to wait. The two boys were running up and down the runway counting the kerosene lanterns, 62 to be exact, marking the path. When the plane came, a generator provided the necessary electricity. And we were off to spend a year in the homeland and share with others the vision we had of evangelizing those we had come to love south of the border.

Chattanooga 1961-1962

Our dear friends at Central Presbyterian Church had secured a nice rental house for us fairly near the church. During that year Frank helped with the music and did some teaching. Of course, we visited all of our supporting churches to let them know what had been accomplished on the field, with many thanks for their generous partnership with us through their gifts. Besides Central Presbyterian, First Presbyterian, Westminster, and East Ridge in Chattanooga there were other supporting churches in Mississippi, Alabama, and Louisiana. Quite often, we would leave the boys with friends, to avoid interrupting their schooling. Sometimes, Frank would go alone, and other times, I would go too, taking the girls with us.

Linda was three and a half and was often the center of attention. Everyone wanted this little "curly-head" to speak Portuguese to them. She was not about to cooperate, however, and started to stutter quite noticeably. After a few weeks, during which I thought we might have a real speech problem on our hands, she quit. Pressure to hear her speak had eased up and she declared one day, "I don't have to go 'da-da-da' anymore." That was the end of her stuttering. Shelley was a happy first-grader, who loved jumping rope. She enjoyed being the "big sister."

Timothy Baird joined our delighted family on Nov. 21, 1961. I had a normal delivery, but he was my heaviest baby. Frank had taken the rest of the family to church for dinner the day before Thanksgiving. He was sharing with someone about Tim's birth and exclaiming about his weight. Another tablemate overheard only part of the conversation and remarked, "Eleven pounds isn't very big for a turkey."

I can remember sitting in my kitchen watching TV almost all day on Feb. 20, 1962, holding my three-month-old baby, the day John Glenn made history as the first American to orbit the earth. In those early days, everyone was amazed at "Space" and the thought of someone actually traveling around the earth in a matter of minutes. We have become very complacent since then and so easily forget the wonder of it all.

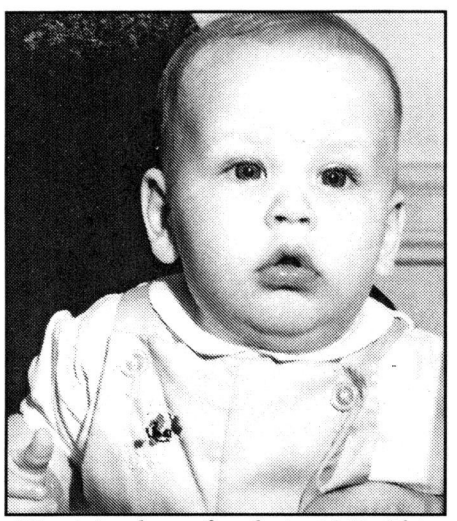

Tim joined our family in 1961. This photo was taken May 27, 1962, when he was 6 months old.

1961 and 1962 were two of the three years when the eight of us lived together. From then on, one or more of the children would be studying away from home. Terry was very active in the Youth Activities of the Presbytery. He was elected Citizenship Chairman for the Presbytery and enjoyed the chance to go to Montreat to a Synod Youth Conference. Dale liked participating with the group at church and won a week at camp for being the top Bible student in 8th grade.

We visited all of our supporters and gave them a closer look as to what was happening on the field. It helped so much to have this personal touch after four years being away in Brazil. Each one could feel more involved in the ministry as they continued to share with their prayers and their support. Sometimes, it was difficult for everyone to catch this vision. We were showing slides in a church once, the first time for us with these people. After the presentation, where Frank had mentioned that Recife was closer to Africa than to New York, an elderly lady had a question. "Mr. Soules, I know you worked in Africa, but what part was it?" We tried to be clearer in the future.

Chattanooga 1961-1962

Finally, the year at home was nearly over and we were looking forward to returning to Crato and the new house that the Mission had purchased. Our sailing date was delayed, so we were able to visit my two sisters in California for three weeks. The cousins had not seen each other for eight years. It was a wonderful mini-reunion which we thoroughly enjoyed.

Frank having fun at a friend's house

Once back in Chattanooga, it was time to say a final goodbye to our many friends. To start our second term in Brazil, once more we took the train to New Orleans. Frank's parents flew in from New York and we spent five days with them. Many

Cousins in California. Front row: Dale, Sharron, Debbie; back row: Danny, Wally and Randy

friends from Natchez and Brookhaven came to wish us *"Boa Viagem"* in addition to those in New Orleans.

We had rented a car, but hadn't allowed sufficient time to return it. Approaching the dock to embark, our progress was impeded by a freight train stopped on the tracks, parallel to the dock. Finally, authorities unbuckled two freight cars and let several of us reach our ship. We barely made it up the gangplank before the ship prepared to leave the dock. However, in the rush to get us and five of our six children on the ship, the keys to the rental car had remained in Frank's pocket. As we held our breath, Frank made a huge effort and successfully threw them over the water to the person responsible for returning the car.

We were excited to be returning to Brazil, but my heart was breaking as the shoreline diminished, seeing Terry, getting smaller and smaller, waving goodbye to us. He would be continuing his last two years of high school at McCallie School in Chattanooga. We were thankful that Spencer and Becky McCallie invited him to live with them. I imagine living in the Headmaster's home had its pros and cons.

Our family in Chattanooga before returning to Brazil.

Second Term Brazil 1962-1966

This trip was much more fun for the family as well as nearly 100 passengers. The ship also carried freight, but there was a swimming pool and lots of recreation opportunities. As a rule, they would not be putting into port at Recife because of the reef, and the resultant delays due to the tides. Because there were thirty three of us disembarking, they made an exception. There was a King Neptune celebration when we passed the equator. All the children on board dressed in costumes and it was very festive. Many acquaintances were begun among the "Mish Kids" (children of missionaries) especially, which have lasted through the years. Timmy turned nine months on the trip, and was adored by all his many "aunts, uncles, and cousins."

I expected coming back for the second time would be easier, because of the familiarity of the sights and sounds. I was

One of many flights on a DC-3

unprepared, however, to be bombarded once again with language I had not used for a year, and some smells that were quite unpleasant. I think I had expected Culture Shock the first time, but not so much on this second arrival. The hustle of getting everything arranged for our trip to Crato involved buying items I knew were not available in the interior.

We hired a truck to transport the barrels and boxes and our family flew on a DC-3 commercial airline the 400 miles to Crato. We arrived on a Sunday and there was no one there to meet us. We assumed they were all busy in their respective duties. It happened that our telegram only reached Mary Garland the week after we arrived, which was pretty much "tudo normal," which means everything is normal, and you had better get used to it. However, we had returned to a transformed city, literally. Hydro-electric power had arrived from the new dam in Paulo Afonso, Bahia, and the neighboring state. Street lights, store fronts showing off TV's, and a general brightness greeted us on our arrival at dusk.

Before we left the States, Frank wanted to arrange for certain items to be sent to us by boat. He secured a box from the local funeral home. This was packed and Joe Smith arranged for a truck from his company to transport it to New Orleans. From there, it went by freighter to Recife, and ultimately to Crato. When the box, being heavy and difficult to handle, was lifted from the truck, it slipped and dropped to the ground; the side opening up like a giant cornucopia. With the contents spread all over the ground, we solicited some help from the neighbors and moved everything into the house. A long trip from Chattanooga to Crato, but the items were much appreciated for many months to come.

Dale and Randy had about two weeks with us and their friends, due to the Ceres school starting late. Both boys had grown about four inches, Dale's was all height, and Randy's was divided between height and width. I began teaching Shelley, and a year later, Linda, using the Calvert course, a new experience for me. I enjoyed it most of the time, and hoped the girls would profit from the quality time together. Linda liked this arrangement better than Shelley. I don't think I was "cut out" to be a teacher, really. Timmy had many "nannies" and "aunties" to make a fuss over him, and he was delighted with the attention. We were back in our adopted country for the next four years, trusting the Lord would direct us and protect us as we labored for Him.

Our second house in Crato

I have always liked pretty, printed sheets, and I had brought some new ones from the States when we returned to Crato. Shortly thereafter, the young girl who was helping me with household chores left and moved to Fortaleza. I soon missed those new sheets, but their whereabouts was a mystery. It was solved when we made a trip to Fortaleza and I saw my very special sheets. Not on a bed, but made into a nice dress which was being worn by my former employee. I guess she thought they were much too pretty to sleep on.

Looking back to our second term, starting in 1962, I remember the relief of having reliable electricity. This influenced many aspects of our lives. We had returned to a new house belonging to the Mission. We could have music playing when we wanted it and lights whenever we turned the switch. Today, it's hard for any of us to imagine what that means, surrounded as we are by modern-day technology. There was no hot running water, of course, so we had an electric shower head which heated the water as it ran through. I never felt very comfortable with that combination of electricity and water, and consequently, always had a dry wash rag in the shower to turn the handle, without which those little shocks were tiny, but not pleasant. I don't know why we put up with that situation the whole time we lived there, but we did.

One time when Shelley and Linda were about 8 and 5 years old, they were taking a shower when they were "joined" by a large aggressive cockroach. Their screams were very vocal as they streaked down the hall to "escape" the intruder. I did become more used to seeing those critters in my house, but I never did like it, doing what I could to eradicate them.

Before long, we had arranged to have screens added to the windows. This was unheard of in Crato, being the first house to "hamper the free flow of air." Brazilians thought it would make the house warmer, which it did to a certain extent, but keeping the fly and mosquito population at bay was worth it. The flies seemed to be worse in this neighborhood, perhaps because the cattle would parade up the street to be slaughtered at a remote location. Each afternoon, the meat was taken to market – I called it the "Hoof to Horn Market."

There was no refrigeration and no aging of beef. Brazilians liked to boil their meat, the usual toughness making it necessary. Thus, they concluded the "filet mignon" cut would fall apart, so they didn't buy it. That worked out fine for us as we usually bought, and prepared, filet every week. We could only buy large pieces of meat and these had to be cut and wrapped for the freezer by the maid. I did my other shopping once a week at a "Feira," the open air market. Vegetables were at a premium, not being appreciated by the local people. Tropical fruit was plentiful, however, which we all enjoyed.

Frank had planted corn and peanuts in the back yard. We also had a bountiful Papaya tree back there in the yard. My children were always complaining that I could hear "everything." Perhaps, in those days, there was some truth to that. One night I mentioned I heard a crunching sound coming from the yard. We investigated and found the leaves of the Papaya tree had been stripped clean by cutter ants. Another time I heard a chewing noise in the bedroom; it turned out to be ants devouring a cardboard box containing my sewing material. This was promptly removed, minus the material, to the backyard and sprayed with an insecticide. Too bad age creeps in and diminishes our faculties of younger years.

This section of town was called "Pimenta" which means pepper. It so happened my name was the same as the verb "to burn" like hot pepper. Frank always got a laugh as he introduced his wife, "Dona Ardy" who lives in "Pimenta." Years later, one of my grandchildren asked the maid if she knew why I was called "Mamaw." Camila's explanation concluded that the name Ardy was so ugly that I didn't like it.

Although electricity was more reliable, the water supply was problematical. Soon after returning to Crato, we learned this first hand. There had been no water when we retired one night. It came on hours later and the kitchen sink had had the stopper left in. This resulted in a flooded situation clear into the dining room by morning. Most of the house had tile floors which helped to keep us cool. It was also easy to mop up and no harm was done except for flooding the drawer under the sink which contained all my spices, brought back to last for the next four years. Of necessity, (being the mother of invention), all the cans were emptied and the contents dried in the sun. Amazingly, this really worked for some, but others were replaced when duplicates could be mailed from the States.

Mail, especially from the States, was often delayed or lost. A classic example of this was a package we received from a couple we barely knew. They had heard us speak shortly before we returned to Brazil, and wanted to send us some cake mixes and other food items. They were also impressed with the need for workers on the field. When we actually received the package, twenty seven months later, they were in Brazil as short-term missionaries!

Linda wrote about some of her experiences of life as a child in Brazil, and it's amazing that some of these things were considered normal. "All of us kids loved going to the interior on the luggage rack of our green Willys Jeep Rural. This was a four-sided rack. Dad would go on evangelical trips to Xique-Xique, Varzea Alegre...and other towns in the Sertão of Ceará. We'd sit on top, bumping along over the dirt roads, getting smacked in the face with passing butterflies and other insects, grabbing cotton from the roadside trees. After awhile, we tired of this adventure and rode the rest of the way inside the vehicle. The only problem was we'd get to places really thirsty, and could only drink boiled water, which was scarce; and the bathroom facilities were sparse." Obviously, I didn't know what was happening on some of these trips.

Jeep Station Wagon "Rural"

One day Randy and two Brazilian passengers were traveling with Frank, and as they drove through the countryside Frank spotted a hawk. He had a keen eye for seeing these birds as he was driving along, and the Brazilian farmers were always grateful for one less hawk to kill their livestock. He stopped the Jeep and asked one of the two men in the back seat to hand him his double barrel 12 gauge shotgun. It was a break-open shotgun, and as Frank closed the gun while it was still pointed inside the Jeep, it must have hit a firing pin and it went off. It blew out the back seat of the vehicle, barely missing the two Brazilians, who were sitting forward. Had they been leaning back in their seats, the result would have been tragic. As Linda wrote about this incident later, she remarked, "I think Dad got nervous that day." I imagine his passengers were even more nervous.

We seemed to be more fully accepted this second term by people in Crato, perhaps because the Mission had built a permanent residence in the town. More importantly, the Vatican II Council under Pope John XXIII opened in 1962. This authorized the use of the mother tongue at Mass and encouraged active participation. They also welcomed with enthusiasm the Ecumenical dialogue with non-catholic Christians. Filtering down to the interior of Brazil, this meant the Priests were teaching the Bible and encouraging their parishioners to read it. It also opened up dialogue with other denominations and persecution of the Protestants was all but eliminated. Frank was even asked to become a member of the Rotary Club in Crato in 1963.

That spring, I took a couple of weeks off and flew to Ceres to visit the boys. I flew as far as Brasília, the new Capital. I took a brief tour by car, and was truly impressed by the work that the missionaries had accomplished there in less than two years. Close to 200 people were attending Sunday school each week in a church outside the Capital. Taking two buses, I arrived in Ceres about 4 ½ hours later. The boys were excited to see me, and also to see the cookies and other goodies I brought. I attended most of their classes and ate in the dining hall with them. On the way home, I went by way of Campinas and had a nice visit with friends at the language school. Of course I did some shopping, and bought two hand-carved lamps of a man and a woman of the interior. These I carried as hand baggage, complete with the shades, on the plane back to Crato. I stopped at Sears in SaõPaulo to see about getting our refrigerator repaired. There was no one in Crato with the expertise, so we actually shipped the motor over 800 miles to have it repaired down south.

By May, 1963, we had supervised the building of an apartment over the garage. This proved to be a wonderful addition, and it was usually occupied, either by missionary colleagues or visitors. Building supervision is always an interesting occupation in Brazil. There were many cases of misunderstanding as well as delays. One time a load of supplies was brought on a donkey cart. When the job was finished, Frank thought he had told the driver he could go ahead and remove the wedges under the cart. Only one vowel separated the word for wedge and pants, however (saying "calça" instead of "calço".) The poor man was taken aback for an instant, but he soon recognized Frank's mistake, and then they all had a good laugh.

The Crato congregation was organized as a church in June with five elders and four deacons. The young pastor was giving excellent leadership.

When Dale and Randy were home during their vacation months, they often joined Frank on trips. In addition to Frank's trumpet, the French horn and trombone provided a brass trio which was enjoyed by all. Dale wanted to do more intensive horn study with Frank, so he stayed in Crato in September when Randy returned to Ceres. Dale continued his high school by correspondence, using the Nebraska Course, and I was, to the best of my ability, still teaching Linda and Shelley.

In August, Frank and I went to Xique-Xique to celebrate Sr. Juca's 50th wedding anniversary. He had been a faithful evangelist for all those years. He was 75 and he and his wife had had 13 children; they weren't sure how many grandchildren – over 50 at least. About 200 people came from other communities. They served rice and chicken on metal plates with soup spoons. No one minded the wait as we were served in shifts.

Sr. Juca and his wife, Dona Maria

Frank and I provided the only music – his trumpet and my playing a little portable organ. They were so grateful that we had come. It had taken about 7 hours to cover the 100 miles, but it was worth it to celebrate their lives and a marriage which had honored the Lord for so many years.

It's amazing now to look back at other things we counted as normal in those days. One instance was the need to have our Jeep repaired. The best mechanic was 6 hours away in another state. Frank took Dale and Randy, driving at night because the

Frank playing trumpet at a meeting, Linda looking in from the window

car overheated so badly. When they arrived in Souza, the mechanic took out the engine and determined what parts were needed. Then Frank and the boys drove Mary Garland's car 250 miles to Recife to obtain these. He left the car for Mary Garland and they brought everything back by bus. The work was completed the next day. Randy was especially interested in what was going on under the hood. Then the three of them drove back to Recife – this time at 25 miles an hour, half the normal speed. During their time in Souza, the trio had played their horns at meetings in the little Presbyterian Church.

In Recife we were looking forward to a little relaxing time at the Mission beach house south of the city. I had flown in with the younger ones to get a check-up for my Rheumatoid Arthritis. After a 5 day mini-vacation, we all returned to Crato. We thoroughly enjoyed those times we spent at the beach. It took us only a few hours by air, but it took Frank and the older boys two days over dirt roads, full of ruts and holes. Even with all the difficulties, it was a good time and we were thankful for family and for safe travel.

On one occasion we were returning from a preaching point with a car full of Brazilians. I was driving the Volkswagen bus which had replaced the old jeep, and we were approaching a barricade between the states. I realized, as I tried to slow down, that I had no brakes. I was informing Frank, rather excitedly, in English, and he was telling me to shift down. Fortunately, the barricade was not across the road, and I was able to shift down sufficiently so that I could pull on the emergency brake. Frank took over, and in the next town the mechanic found air in the brake line. I was very thankful for the peaceful end of a harrowing experience. The occupants probably did not know the full extent of this scenario.

In November, our nation was shocked to its core, and it was felt around the world. Let me quote from a letter I wrote on Nov. 28, 1963.

Second Term Brazil 1962-1966

"Graduating" to a Volkswagen Bus

On that fateful day of Nov. 22, 1963, two hours after the hate of one man had completely shocked the world, a man died here in Crato also. As sickness had weakened him for weeks, his death did not come as such a terrific shock. Sr. Aminadabe was only three years older than John Kennedy and left a wife and thirteen children. His youngest was the age of Caroline Kennedy. The news of his death did not go out over the radio, nor were there any special TV broadcasts made in his honor. Few people outside Crato and the neighboring city knew him in life or knew of his death. And yet, so much more important, God knew him. He was his child. He was buried the next day and as I walked behind the group of mourning friends and relatives to the cemetery, I felt that there were many in the procession who had never heard that a person who dies in Christ can have peace without any fear. Aminadabe was not well-to-do but he made a substantial living for his family by running a good mechanic shop. ...As *three or four hundred people, many who were not Christians, paid their last respects, they heard music and a message of hope perhaps for the first time. … Perhaps in his death, he was more of a testimony than he had been in his life.*

As 1964 began, the political situation was getting much more tense and the work of some of our colleagues was threatened. On March 31st, by the grace of God, Brazil's military was able to avert a Communist takeover of the country. No blood was shed, but it had come very close to a revolution. Money had been printed and "hit lists" were discovered, with some missionary names included.

In May, 1964, our oldest graduated from High School. We were sorry not to be present, but were happy to have him return to Crato after such a long time. Terry planned to delay his entrance to college for a year and part of that year was spent in Crato and part in Recife.

The congregation was growing in Juazeiro and we had the opportunity to purchase a piece of land on the main street. It wasn't much in American currency, but in Brazil, it was a big commitment. It was a real testimony to the faith of the believers in that town, and their desire for a place of worship.

Later that summer, Frank had a hernia operation in Crato. I remember taking him all his meals and staying overnight with him. The menu at the hospital was fat-laden the way the Brazilians liked it. He recovered well, but we all missed his trumpet music for a few months.

Iracy and Deusanira, daughters of a worker in Xique-Xique, came to live with us. They both were taking advantage of attending high school in Crato. They did some baby-sitting and helped with the household chores, which I really appreciated. They both went on to further their education in Garanhuns and Recife. Later, they married and raised their own families. Iracy is the wife of a pastor in Bahia, and I have had occasion to see her various times on my visits to Brazil.

Terry was teaching some English and helping with translation that Frank did for the Rotary Club. Terry expressed his frustration in a letter written at that time, "If I don't emerge from this that I do not understand, this time of life of mine, I will at least emerge a bitter critic of poor writing, the ignored but yet spoken cliché, the cute clever and thoroughly sad, the purple passages of inebriated prose." This was not an easy year for him, but he had certainly learned to express himself on paper, at least. As an adult, he has published two small books of poetry and done extensive work translating *Dante's Divine Comedy*. He is translating the first part, *The Inferno*, at present, into rhymed vernacular English. He hopes to finish this and the last two parts within a few years.

During this time, the Cariri valley, including Crato and Juazeiro, came into the news in an interesting fashion. A U.C.L.A. engineering professor, Morris Asimow, started a project in 1962 to organize small corporations that would benefit the Brazilians.

He brought graduate students and professors from U.C.L.A. down to our area. We became involved because he asked a master mechanic from Indiana to come and teach for six months. John Cook and his wife were both 72 and were living in the mosquito-infested hotel in town when I returned from Recife. I had been temporarily staying with the teen-age kids in Recife until the Board approved our going there as dorm parents for a few months. I knew John

Crato Palace Hotel

and Charlotte would not last six months under those conditions and we invited them to occupy our apartment over the garage and board with us.

He did a remarkable job teaching, even with his nearly non-existent Portuguese. They were a sweet couple and they loved to become surrogate grandparents to Timmy. They made a lasting impression on my family, however, in a much different manner. John had been "hen-pecked" for so many years, he didn't even realize it. At each meal we would invariably hear, "Eat, John, eat." Apparently, she thought this was a necessary ingredient to his nutrition.

The project did much for our area, and Asimow was able to organize five separate corporations to mill corn and to make shoes and transistor radios, as well as structural ceramics and pressed wood. He hired local managers and raised money so that there were, eventually, all-Brazilian boards and local land owners. He came back the next summer and organized a cement plant, a dairy, and a meat-processing plant. The U.S. agreed to back similar projects all over Latin America. These were given a name, with the initials, RITA, Rural Industrial Technical Assistance. This did a great deal for the economy of our area. [Information from a "Time" article, Aug. 14, 1964]

Frank turned 40 in November, 1964, and I wanted to invite many of his friends to help him celebrate. Hulda, the wife of our evangelist, Josafá, helped me write the dialog to go along with slides, and I presented "This is your Life." It was fun, and a lot of work, to put together all the slides to show his life. Of course, I did not have any of his early days, but there were many from the time we met up to the time in Brazil. When the apartment was built over the garage, a large white square had been painted on the driveway wall. This, along with seating on the steps behind the house, made a good amphitheater. We could project the slides on the wall, which worked out very well. He was thrilled and everyone enjoyed a great party. The Brazilians loved getting a picture of our early life in the States.

A change of residence, temporarily, began for us in March, 1965. A new American School had been opened the year before in Recife. The Mission finally agreed to establish a student home there to enable the "mish kids" to attend an accredited high school. A house was purchased and we were assigned to the position of dorm parents to get it started. This was only until a couple could be approved for this job on a permanent basis. The mission was reluctant to remove an evangelistic couple from the field, but agreed to it for a few months. The American School of Recife – EAR ("Escola Americana do Recife") - enrolled about 240 students in twelve grades in a city of a million people. It provided quality education for families in diplomatic, industrial, and military as well as in missionary service.

Having a home for children of missionaries in a city where they could study and be better prepared for college met a felt need on the mission field. On a personal note, it was a big plus for us to have all six of our kids living with us. It was the last time this would happen. The house was not large, but there was a room out back that was adequate to sleep four boys. The school was only three blocks from the house, and much of the time we attended church services held at the school also. I had a nice big kitchen and I loved baking for such an appreciative "crew."

In July, we returned to Crato with the three youngest, and I resumed the Calvert Course with Shelley and Linda. I wrote in one of our missionary letters that I had more fun cooking for ten than teaching two. Frank took over the responsibility of pastoring the Crato church while Edijece was studying in Richmond, Virginia.

By the time we moved to Recife, the Prof. Natanael Cortez School was being used more and more. There was a night course where Bible was taught and a Practical Worker's course. This was in addition to English that was already being offered. Frank had been involved in counselor and follow-up training for the evangelistic campaigns to be held later in Recife and Brasília.

When the school year started in 1965, a couple had not been approved as yet to come to Recife as dorm parents. So I took Shelley and returned to Recife for a few more months as a dorm parent at the hostel. I was back in Crato for Christmas with my family. The Stoffels came in January, 1966 to take over the position permanently.

Randy was not too pleased with the new house parents, due to a personality clash, apparently. As a grown man, he has told me of some of the pranks he and another student played on them. Some nights, they would sneak out and go to the beach where the balsa fishing rafts (*jangadas*) were resting. They would actually take them out into the ocean – no motor – no sail – and no light. It must have been quite an adventure for two young boys. They always brought them back and rolled them up on the beach. Apparently, they were never caught, either by the fishermen or the Stoffels. Another time they painted the stepping stones silver.

Dale went with a group from EAR, who flew to Belém and took a boat up the Amazon River to the city of Manaus. This is where the famous Opera House was built when Rubber was "King." Dale was interested in folk-lore, and at each stop along the river, he would collect items reflecting Brazilian history in the area. In Santarém he found many American-sounding names on gravestones. He was told these represented southerners from the States who had settled in that region after the Civil War. They were called the "Confederados in the Amazon." His report about this trip was very interesting.

Terry had been accepted at the University of Pennsylvania, and he was looking forward to college. He chose to make an adventurous trip home instead of flying straight there. This involved some hitch-hiking, some buses and other inexpensive transportation. He was able to visit the capital cities of Bolivia, Peru, Ecuador, Columbia and most of the Central American countries. He actually visited the very famous ruins of Machu

Second Term Brazil 1962-1966

Pichu, but not wanting to give the appearance of a tourist, he took no camera. How disappointing to have no pictorial record of a fascinating trip. He did feel badly he had not written more about the trip en route (we received a letter, a postcard and a telegram in over 2 months) so he made us a tape recording when he visited his grandparents over the holidays. Unfortunately, that cassette was lost in the mails, thus many of the memories have been erased over time.

Fern Snider was using her gifts as she prepared aids and orientation for the teachers in Crato and in the field. She was doing a lot of traveling and overseeing two Sunday Schools in the poor sections of Crato. She was a much loved and appreciated colleague.

In November, 1965, Frank was in Natal, the capital of Rio Grande do Norte, the state north of us, helping with a ten-day evangelistic campaign. He was part of a team to train 50 counselors for this campaign. It was so encouraging to see 214 people make decisions for Christ and see a renewed unity among the evangelical churches. 14 young people volunteered for Christian service. Frank was also one of four speakers at a 3-day seminar for pastors. About 400 pastors attended.

In those days, Crato did not have a good variety of vegetables, like we had become accustomed to in Recife. I prevailed upon Randy to go regularly to the market in Recife and buy a week's supply. These he would take to the airport and ask the pilot, a friend of ours, to deliver them to Juazeiro. We were more than happy to receive them on our end and thus improve our diet. Before long, the Japanese had moved into the Cariri valley, including Crato, and started planting many kinds of vegetables. These they introduced into the market place, and gradually educated the Brazilians in more healthful nutrition. That same pilot was flying the plane I was in another time. He came back to my seat and asked me to look at the other side where the propeller was not rotating. He calmly told me, "See, I told you these planes could fly with just one motor." I was glad to know we were headed back to Recife.

The boys came home from Recife for Christmas and we had a full house, to be sure. We had met the Hawbakers through the American School where their children attended. That Christmas, their children were studying in the U.S. and we invited George and Libby to join us in Crato. He worked with the Rural Industrial Development Project under USAID. I still keep in touch with them.

I had arranged to have our turkey roasted at a bakery in town – theirs with the only electric ovens. Mine was much too small. On the 24th, I discovered these ovens had not been working for three days. I found another bakery with wood ovens willing to do me this favor, but they were doing a regular baking on Christmas, so we could only start the process about 3:00 p.m. Our dinner began at 8:30, and by then our appetites were well prepared. Fern was with us, as well as the Cooks, and another man from the Asimow project. It was a memorable Christmas and no one minded the delayed dinner hour.

The Watch Night Service was very special that year, when we heard two youngsters and six adults, recently converted, give their testimonies. After the service, another young man indicated his desire to accept Christ as his Savior.

Many years after their daring adventure, Randall relayed to me the extent of his travels with Bill Brown, a fellow student. He had come to Crato with him for the holidays, and they decided they would go visit the Davis family, about 600 miles to the northwest. Some friends offered a little financial help in return for "something unique" from the interior.

The boys only knew that the Davis family lived by a bridge over the Tocantins River, which eventually flows into the Amazon. Their basic means of transportation was on cotton trucks and buses. This was decidedly a "low-budget" affair, and they ate very little on the 6-day trek to the port on the river. Sometimes truckers would buy them a meal. They reached the port but didn't have enough money for the boat fare. Buying two bundles of long sticks, which they tied together with rope, they made a makeshift raft. Two sticks were saved out to be used as paddles. They bought 11 bananas, and set the raft adrift at sunset. The river widened and for a short while they could barely see the lights on either shore. They even slept some, which seems quite remarkable, on a river filled with "people-eating" creatures.

With luck and an overworked "guardian angel," they paddled to shore when they saw the bridge and arrived at the Davis home. They joined three of the Davis clan, and had a rollicking good time for a few days, which included jumping off the cliff into the river several times. They borrowed some money to pay for passage on the "African Queen" vintage boat back to the port, taking with them three live *coatis* (small raccoons) tucked into their leather water bags. From there, they flew home. They triumphantly arrived with no mishap, presenting their "prizes" to their benefactors. The animals were accepted eventually by the American School of Recife. Any travel in subsequent years was tame after "reaching the Tocantins."

I had hepatitis in January, 1966 with a relapse in late February. I was too weak to teach both girls, so our colleagues, the Perkins, graciously agreed to keep Shelley with them in Recife so she could finish 5th grade at EAR. I continued teaching Linda, but for over a month I was in bed. Most of the family had suffered from this disease by then, but it seems I was hit the hardest.

There are so many loose ends to settle when one is leaving an area after eight years. There was much sorting and packing, even more difficult because of the uncertainty of our location on our return. Frank had to turn over the work to the new pastor, Rev. Domingos Andrade Lima. How thankful we were to have him and his family here in the newly acquired manse.

There was the trauma of saying goodbye to our friends in Crato and Juazeiro. Before leaving Recife for our year's Home Assignment, we had the privilege of seeing Dale graduate from EAR. He had been a busy senior as Vice President of his class and editor of the school paper. He was thrilled to be accepted at Yale on a partial scholarship in the fall.

I was doing quite a bit of sewing and planned to make a nice dress to wear at home. I took Tim shopping with me as I was deciding on material. He heard the saleslady mention the price of a meter of cloth, and exclaimed, "Um futebol por metro." You get the idea. He was shocked that he could get a soccer ball for the same price as a yard of cloth. He was already very much into soccer.

For this furlough, we planned to take some large items home to stay, which we had found we did not need in Brazil. These were packed in four steel drums to be shipped by freight when transportation was available. A huge flood hit that area a couple of days before we were to leave, and did great damage to the storeroom where we had our barrels. Everything was soaked. We postponed our trip by three days and emptied the barrels. I remember much could not be salvaged, but we tried very hard to dry out photos and slides which could not be replaced. Insurance paid to replace some items, but when everything arrived in the US months later, the smell of mildew was overpowering. Most of those photos were shown, however, as we visited our churches that year.

Chattanooga
1966-1967

On our way home, we stopped off in Tampa to visit Frank's cousin, Harold Soules and his family. The men had gone ahead to the car with the bags, and Jo (his wife) and I were following with the three children. I happened to glance down, saying, "Someone dropped their tickets." I picked them up, thinking to turn them in, I guess, when I discovered they were our tickets. They had dropped out of Frank's pocket – not only the tickets to Chattanooga, but also the return ones to Brazil. "Curiosity may have killed the cat," but I'm glad I just didn't walk on by.

In June, we visited Frank's parents when we took Randy to his summer job at Camp-of-the-Woods. We were able to work in one full, exciting day at Expo '67 in Montreal. Randy was especially interested in Buckminster Fuller's Geodesic Dome. It was a thrill to be there.

The summer in Chattanooga was filled with shopping and visits to dentists and doctors. Both Dale and Randy were working at Camp-of-the-Woods in the Adirondacks, NY. In July, Central Presbyterian Church had their first World Missions Convocation and it was a privilege to be with more than 160 fellow missionaries, staff and Board Members. For one week we met together, considering our mission in today's world. Later that summer we took a vacation trip to visit Frank's folks and the boys. We also saw Terry in Pennsylvania, and enjoyed New York, Boston and Williamsburg on the way home. It was not only great to visit so many friends and relatives, but the ease of travel on American highways was a real change from what we had become accustomed to in Brazil. In the fall, things settled into a routine of sorts, with Frank preaching most every Sunday in one of the churches in the area. He needed to do work on his Master's thesis during the week. I kept more than busy, taking care of the house and family. I had been used to having help in Brazil, but not having the frustrations that went along with the help made the transition easier here in the States. Randy was 17 and was going to Brainerd High. Shelley was our Girl Scout and Linda, at eight, enjoyed being a Brownie. Timmy attended the kindergarten at Central Pres. and was loved by everyone. That Christmas was very special with Terry home from University of Pennsylvania and Dale from Yale. Shortly afterwards, Frank entered the hospital for a tonsillectomy which slowed him down for a while. It's not easy for an adult to go through experiences that should have been taken care of years before.

Third Term Brazil 1967-1969

A few months later, we were headed back to Brazil, to Campinas for a three-month refresher course in Portuguese. Frank was pleased to be taking a new trumpet back. This time we traveled by air since travel was becoming less expensive to fly than to go by boat. We flew into SaõPaulo and once again found ourselves at the Language School, catching up on a language that has a way of disappearing with lack of use.

I don't know how Frank was able to study Portuguese at all, because it seemed every waking moment was spent writing his Thesis. It was a long process, tracing the doctrine of the image of God in man. He often brought gleanings of insights to the table, and Shelley commented once, "I'll be able to write a thesis when I get to college without even doing the research." Frank was so focused on finishing this, that everything else was eliminated; he even stopped shaving, to save X number of minutes a day. When I went out to a movie or a restaurant, it was with girlfriends.

Our supporting churches had raised the money for a new Volkswagen Microbus which we bought in Campinas. It was wonderful to have good, reliable transportation and we were very appreciative. By December, we had finished the Refresher Course and Frank had completed most of the writing of his thesis. It was a big help to have this extra push in the language as we began our third term, in Recife.

After Christmas in Campinas, we drove north with the three youngest children. We now had half our family studying in the States. It was not easy for them to be so far away. During his senior year at Brainerd High in Chatttanooga, Randy

Leaving Campinas with our younger three

was living with our good friends, the Morrows. He enjoyed using his soccer-style kick to help the football team with extra points. He was even recognized in the paper for this talent. Dale was at Yale and Terry was at University of Pennsylvania.) We spent two nights in Rio, and had the thrill of going up *"Pão de Açúcar,"* the famed Sugar Loaf Mountain.

Later on, when we visited a sugarcane processing plant in Pernambuco, the origin of that name was explained to us. The cane syrup, after being boiled to the right consistency, is poured into a large cone. This has a spigot on the bottom to drain off any impurities. When this hardens, the sugar cone (sugar loaf) is removed and inverted. The shape resembles the "mountain" to some degree.

It took us three more days to reach Salvador, where we spent New Year's Eve and New Year's Day. So far it had been all paved roads, until we reached Juazeiro, another city in Bahia. From there to Crato the roads were in bad shape. We spent a week sorting our belongings and having meetings in Várzea

Alegre and in Crato. The road to Recife had been improved somewhat, but it still took over 12 hours. We needed to find a house to rent before our things could be shipped from Crato. We moved into one a ways back from the beach, until July. We had a large dog while we lived there, and that dog could not stand to hear the trumpet. He would make a whining sound and have to be put outdoors any time Frank was practicing.

Our primary responsibility in Recife would be to help the evangelical churches to reach the new-literates for Christ. In cooperation with the local Presbytery, evangelistic home Bible studies were started in the middle and upper-class area of Recife.

By April, 1968, Frank was able to finish the final draft of his thesis. The finished copy was presented and accepted for the Master of Theology degree granted by Columbia Seminary in June. The 220-page thesis was longer than many doctoral theses. He was so thankful to have it completed.

Frank's father passed away in June, and it was hard to be so far from his mom. We were able to talk to her by "ham" radio which helped some. It was a comfort to know he was a believer, and not like so many in Brazil who "die without hope."

Randy graduated from Brainerd High in June. He and Bob Morrow were to visit us for the month of August. Tragically, Bob was killed by a hit-and-run driver as the boys were riding bikes in the Florida Keys before they were to fly to Brazil the next day. It was a sad realization when Randy disembarked alone and told us what had happened. Terry was also with us for a few weeks before returning to the University of Pennsylvania. Both Terry and Randy left the end of August for the States. Randy entered the University of Virginia that fall. To have three boys in college at once was challenging to say the least. We were proud of their accomplishments and wanted each one to succeed and be fulfilled.

In July, we moved to a house on the beach. We called it the "House with the Blue Tower," because of the blue, elevated water tank. It was so distinctive; we had to give it a name. There

Linda, Tim and Shelley on a jangada

are other things that stand out in my mind while we lived there. For one thing, it was on Beira Mar, or Shore Drive. That was on the ocean side of the street. Across the street, with different numbering, it was called Bernardo Vieira de Melo. Even postmen would get confused as to the location of a certain house.

Houses were built adjacent to each other with no entrance to the back yard except through the house. The septic tank was in the back yard and had to be cleaned once while we lived there. This meant the hose from the tank to the truck went through the living room. I mentioned to the workers that there was a weak spot in the hose which should be taken care of. They ignored me and started the process. Shortly thereafter, the bubble burst and the contents being pumped were no longer contained by the hose; splattering the floor and the chair legs and making a smelly mess. Fortunately, there were no rugs or curtains. As I remember, they didn't apologize, but did continue with another hose. I didn't keep my cool, I'm afraid. The next day was Tim's 7th birthday and the smell of Pine Sol permeated the house, which was better than the alternative. The party was enjoyed by all, oblivious to the catastrophe of the day before.

For months I was not comfortable driving in Recife because of the congestion. Finally, I ventured out and became more used to the traffic, but never really felt at ease. Perhaps we should never feel at ease in traffic.

In September, 1968, Frank made a quick trip to the States. To strengthen the work with the leaders in Recife, he was given the opportunity to visit Washington, D.C. and see the Christian Leadership work being done among the members of Congress. They were involved with the Prayer Breakfast Movement. When he visited his mother in New York, he was asked to officiate at her marriage to Lee Barnes, an old friend who had lost his mate earlier that year. This was quite a surprise, but truly a wonderful time of joy for them both.

By Christmas that year, we were opening up a previously untouched area of the city, Boa Viagem, working with Pierre and Lois DuBose. This was a more affluent section of society, but the need of the truth of the gospel was the same as in the poorer sections. There was a new housing project on the outskirts of the city and we took part in the first Presbyterian services for the people who lived there. Among the affluent families, there was no lack of material things, so it was difficult for them to see spiritual needs in their lives. In contrast, the poorer families had little in the material sense, and were usually more open to messages which gave them hope for the future. Music gave us an entrance in both cases, and Frank was endeavoring to "be all things to all men so that by all possible means [he] might save some" like Paul. (I Cor. 9:22) Both were growing. It was wonderful to see what an open spirit can do to break down barriers and help people see their own faults and needs.

1969 was a most interesting year and full of new aspects of our ministry. Frank had started meeting with some evangelicals to pray about a weekly prayer luncheon. In March, they were joined by elder Torquato Marques dos Santos. Jule Spach had been working in Brasília and brought two of the members from Brasília's Congressional Prayer Luncheon to visit Recife. This helped to start a prayer luncheon with about 12 leaders in the city joining Sr. Torquato and Frank. He wrote in a letter to our supporters, "I am very happy to be working with Brazilian men in a way I have never been able to before, and, at the same time, see relationships with other missionaries deepening. I have much to thank God for."

Iracy, who had lived with us in Crato, continued her studies in Recife. Caldeman was also studying there to prepare for the ministry. They fell in love and were to be married in Xique-Xique. She had been raised there and wanted Frank to perform the ceremony where her family and friends were. Before the ceremony in the church, the law required a civil ceremony first. However, all the judges in her district were to go on vacation at the same time, so she and Caldeman had to actually be married a week before their ceremony at home.

They expected lots of people to attend, so her father built a lean-to addition to the kitchen. Tim was quite engrossed in watching the slaughtering of animals, a first for him. If I'm not mistaken, Iracy's father killed a pig, a cow, and several chickens. The ceremony was simple, but very nice. Afterwards, we were served a wonderful meal. They only had one table, so twelve at a time were served, the plates were washed and the next group was seated. We slept in hammocks that night, covering our heads with a sheet to avoid the mosquitoes.

Dale joined us for about four months and took a course in the Federal University.

Frank had an office in the center of town in an evangelical bookstore. This gave him an opportunity to minister to pastors and students who came by, and to counsel people in spiritual distress who visited the bookstore. He was able to produce, with help from some Brazilians, an eight-page booklet in Portuguese on "Christ's Man Today." It was sent to all our Brazil missionaries and given to a number of Brazilians.

In addition to other responsibilities, we again added "House Parents" to our job description. There was a "mish kid" from São Luiz and one from Brasília who needed a place in the Student Hostel. They joined us and our three younger children. Both Frank and I enjoyed teaching English to some Brazilians.

The Board approved a three-month's furlough for us in December 1969. This was a special blessing with the three older boys in the States. Missionaries were no longer required to be on the field four years before a furlough. Because of that change, we could go home more often, but stay a shorter time.

It was very special to have Christmas with our entire family together. Terry and Dale wanted to give us a poster they worked on until the wee hours of Christmas morning. They took the first two verses of Revelation 22, and Terry translated them from the Greek and wrote it out in English and Portuguese, as well as the Greek. Dale wrote it in beautiful calligraphy. Terry said these three languages "would encompass Dad's world." It was a much-appreciated gift. That was the year it snowed and gave us a "White Christmas." An extra bonus!!

Fourth Term Brazil 1969-1973

Terry successfully completed his four years at the University of Pennsylvania. He had met Virginia (Ginny) Gerhardt there, who was a student in the School of Medicine. They were married in June 1970 in a garden ceremony. Dale and Randy represented the family, as we were unable to be there. After a camping adventure out west, the newlyweds were back in time for Ginny to start her 3rd year in medical school. Terry was working in a bookstore and putting together their experiences on their trip for his own book. Dale and Randy also drove out west that summer, delivering a car to San Francisco for Ron McBride, a friend of theirs. They had even toyed with the idea of back-packing their way down the Pan-American Highway from there, and across to Brazil. Plans changed, and Dale stayed and worked awhile in Arizona, and Randy returned to college in Virginia.

That summer, we were excited to watch the World Cup Soccer matches on our own TV. When Brazil plays, the whole country watches, and when they win, as they did for the third time in 1970, the country erupts in one unanimous celebration. Tim could read the "Ao Vivo" sign on the TV, indicating live telecast. He wanted an explanation, however, and wondered if they were still alive after being knocked down. We had also been in Brazil in 1958 and 1962 when they brought home the Cup, and it was thrilling to watch the famous Pelé on all three occasions. Frank and Tim went to see Pelé play in Recife in 1971.

Frank wrote in a letter home in 1970, "I am more and more conscious that here in Brazil people in and out of the churches are hungry for something real – as hungry as the taxi driver whose conversation revealed his openness to God. Right in front of my house we bowed our heads and he gladly accepted Christ as his Savior and Lord!"

We continued to serve as House Parents. Ann Spach and Paulo Leão graduated that year and Jean Williams was in her senior year. With all these teenagers listening to their "favorite" records, sometimes it was hard to "squeeze" in some from our generation. We tried to fill the gap in little ways here and there. Cooking helped!!

Recife's Christian Leadership Group continued to be a challenge and an inspiration to Frank. As a suggestion from one of the members, they began reading a chapter from the Bible each time they met. There was continued spiritual growth, and in November, 1970, they had the first Governor's Prayer Luncheon. About 40 officials attended, as well as the Governor and Governor-elect.

The leaders in Brasília desired the Recife group to take more initiative in starting leadership meetings in four nearby state capitals. As the Prayer Luncheons continued, they invited their wives to join them at Christmas, Easter and Mother's Day. Frank described this joint meeting in a letter written in May. "Wives of such leaders as the medical director of a hospital, the head of the state teachers' college, a banker, the local superintendent of the federal railroad, and the head of the federal medical school here are showing increasing interest in getting together on a fellowship basis. One remarked to Ardy, 'We need to get back to God and the Bible'…Other joint meetings are in the offing. By the end of the year we hope the women will also want to meet regularly, with the purpose of becoming better acquainted with Christ and with each other."

In our Christmas letter in 1970, I quoted a poem my Mother had written years before. I quoted it again in 2005, not remembering the previous time. It was still applicable.

" 'Where can I find Christmas?' a weary traveler cried…
'In the living room of nations, there is no warmth inside.

*The confusion of the people reflects the drive for gold;
The fireplace burns with deadly hate and still the hearth is cold.'

The Prince of Peace then answered, 'Stay, do not depart...
And you will find your Christmas in the birthplace of your heart.'
And all the chimes of Heaven will join the songs on earth,
When you make room for Jesus and celebrate His birth."*

Randy joined us in Recife at the beginning of 1971. He had taken a year off from college and had been working in Chattanooga. The owner of the bus company in Recife was a good friend of ours. He arranged for Randy to work as a supervisor in the maintenance garage for a period of four months. He studied the manual on the trip down to Brazil and did a great job. The workers asked him if he were an American, and his answer was that he "descended from Americans." He thought they might lose respect if they found out he was an American college kid. His Portuguese didn't give him away. He learned a lot during that period.

Quite often groups from churches in the south would visit us and other areas where there was mission work. One such group came from Virginia, and for recreation, we went swimming at the beach – something they couldn't do in the winter in the states. As we were jumping the waves, one of the ladies and I were talking about where we grew up. We discovered, to our amazement, that we were both from California and had been in Nurses training in the same hospital. Her sister had even been in my class.She had married one of the veterans she cared for in the hospital, and I had married a man who grew up 3000 miles from my home town. We live in a truly mobile society.

We desired to reach out to the youths in this upper-class district. Many were children of Brazilian Air Force personnel. We were led to rent a large, old house which would be suitable for this ministry. Youth groups from evangelical churches began to use the center for special outings. We had a volleyball court with lighting provided by one of the men in the Leadership Group. We rented this house with its coconut grove for only a year, because funds were very limited. We called it the LINK (or "ELO".) We began to offer English lessons and to have informal get-togethers to discuss relevant issues and share music. Frank even moved his office there from the center of town. We needed Brazilian youths to form a team to help us in this endeavor. Several were chosen for this team and they chose the motto: "To come to know the Lord Jesus better and to make Him known."

In February, 1971, we celebrated our Silver Anniversary with four of the children joining in. How our lives had changed over those 25 years. We had a simple reception at our residence, and I did most of the baking. There were informal messages given by some in the Leadership Group and by the young people in the LINK club. Elder Torquato Santos had a wonderful prayer. We had so much to be thankful for.

In May, a flood invaded the Student Home. As this had happened before, the Mission decided to sell it, even though

Celebrating 25 years with Shelley, Randy and Linda (and Tim, who was already asleep when this photo was taken.)

it was close to the school. Some things stand out in my mind related to that flood. It was necessary for us to move out that summer. We put every bit of furniture that could conceivably be elevated on blocks, even the refrigerator. This served the purpose so we lost very little. Timmy was sick

An Air Force Lt. coming to help after the flood

with a high fever the night of the flood, so we put him on a cot in our room. He was better in the morning and looked around his bed, surrounded by water, and declared, "I'll have lots to tell at 'Show and Tell' at school." Water had not receded outside either, and a friend of ours, in the Brazilian Air Force, came up to the front door in a rubber raft wondering what we might need. He soon returned with medicine for Timmy and hot bread from the bakery for all of us. By evening, all that was left was a muddy mess all over the floor, and on our Volkswagen engine which had to be repaired. We had failed to park it on the slanting driveway with the engine side elevated.

Our annual Regional Meeting was held in June that year in Natal, a beautiful location on the ocean. This was the capital of Rio Grande do Norte where they had held the evangelistic campaign in 1966.

Sue Fisher arrived in time to go with us to the Regional Meeting and help with her musical talents in the children's Bible School. Sue was the daughter of our dear friends, Ruth and Ben, from Norwich Corners days. Her parents were quite worried when she had not answered their page in the Miami Airport. They were finally able to talk with her in Recife and be assured she was fine. She said, "Yes, I heard the page, but I didn't think I was that Sue Fisher."

In July, we moved into a house, temporarily, that belonged to the Mayerinks who worked for the Philips Company. The lovely beach property came with a "price." It was our responsibility to care for a rabbit, a turtle, two dogs, and other animals, as well as a parrot that chewed the awning and woke us rudely at 5:00 a.m., every day!! Between us, we kept the "menagerie" fed and cared for, but the maid who came with the house gave me more emotional trauma than any hired help I had encountered up to that time. She kept us well fed, but her personality was in "clash mode" all the time.

We enjoyed Sue's musical talent on the piano that summer, and combined with Sally's guitar and Frank's trumpet, it made a contribution in church services and at the LINK club. Sally Steger was spending the summer with the Brandts. We missed Sue when she returned to Hartwick College in Oneonta, New York.

In September, 1971, we received our new 1972 Microbus and the next day Frank went to Crato to be there for the first anniversary of the dedication of the new sanctuary. A seminarian, Aírton Borges, Elder Josafá Santos, and Cilas Cunha went with him. This visit gave renewed courage to the Crato pastor who for nearly two years had labored in this difficult city. The meetings and the trip were a blessing to all of them.

The first week of October, Frank had to put his trumpet away for a few months due to a second hernia operation. By November we had to let the Link house go because of financial considerations. This meant that the piano was back in our house, and the ping pong table on our back porch. We were in another rented house across the highway from the beach. Meetings, music and young people were a regular mix in filling up the house.

There were many pieces of God's puzzle falling into place because of and through our move. Two specialists in reaching non-church kids were scheduled to come from SaõPaulo to spend a month with us over the holidays. Edgard and Adilson came to live with us as there was no longer the possibility of staying at the Link club. This was to be my "down-time" when the kids from the hostel left for vacation. I really didn't want two "extras" here over Christmas. But, after praying about it, I agreed that if it could reach our Shelley, who was turning away from all things spiritual, it would certainly be worth any sacrifice. After a week or so, Beto and Cilas moved in with us also, to get more training with the men from the south.

With adequate supervisors in the house, Frank and I spent an overnight at the mission beach house. That was the night a robber climbed up the outside of the porch to the second floor. He entered our bedroom, took drawers out into the light and stole all of my jewelry that was worth anything. Even so, we were thankful that none of the children had wakened and startled the thief. His lookout, we were told later, was across the street with a gun. Perhaps he was armed also. We never recovered my lovely Brazilian stones or the record player, but having the family safe was much more important.

Even though this event was upsetting, the month turned out to be a blessing to many of the kids in Recife, as well as to our family. Edgard and Adilson asked Shelley if she wanted to attend their camp near Campinas for a week. It meant she would be a week late starting school and she agreed. As there were no additional bus reservations available, Frank was willing to drive them over 1000 miles to Campinas. One of the young men was used to driving a Volkswagen bus, so the two took turns and drove straight through – a 40 hour trip. This made it possible for Beto to go with them also. While Shelley was at camp, Frank went to a Brazilian Campus Crusade for Christ training in Santos, on the coast.

That week was momentous in Shelley's spiritual life, and she made a decision for Christ while there. Her rebellious spirit had been replaced by a willingness to serve and a desire to learn more about the Lord. Very often, children have to hear God's voice from a different perspective from that of a parent.

Frank needed another driver to accompany him on the return trip. On Sunday, he asked if there was anyone who would like to go to Recife with him. One young man came to him after church, to say his uncle had given him a one-way bus ticket from Recife and he'd be glad to help out. The Lord is never late in providing our needs. Back in Recife, Frank trained Cilas and Beto in using the Four Spiritual Laws. They went out on the beach, talking to young people, and over half of those spoken to would make decisions to accept Christ.

More and more young people were aware of the meetings in our home, where there was always a lot of music and a lot of food. Their favorites were my cakes and sandwiches made with my homemade mayonnaise. These meetings were usually on Saturday, and later on Sunday, when Cilas would give a brief message and Beto would lead in games and sports. Beto was very knowledgeable in electrical subjects. He helped Tim to build a crystal radio set, which made a big hit.

My heart had to be worked on during this time. Usually, I would "escape" to the Mission beach house, about two miles away, for some peace and quiet. My trip to the states, to attend Explo '72 in Dallas, was approved by the Board. This was put on by Campus Crusade for Christ. After returning, I had a different attitude, and I wanted to be more a part of the activities. I was joining in whenever the young people came. I even learned to play chess, so I could find some common ground with those who came. I played a fair game of ping-pong, too. I began to like the music and the non-stop activity. There were usually 35 or 40 kids present. I'm so thankful that I didn't miss the opportunity to be a part of this area of our ministry. In a letter home, I wrote, "Isn't God good to work out all the details?

Our extended family, from left, Jeannie, Shelley; 2nd row, David, Duncan and Chuck; top, Linda and Tim

How come we're so stubborn to believe this, when we can't see the answers?" Shelley became part of the music team with her guitar, and Linda and the four "mish kids" Jeannie Williams, Duncan Lindsay, Dave Arnold and Chuck Clark who lived with us, joined in also. Outside the home, I served as president of the American Women's Association of Recife and on the American Community Church Board.

All of these young Brazilians were from nominally Roman Catholic homes. Some came at other times to study English or participate in Bible studies which Frank or Cilas conducted. When school started in the fall, Shelley wanted to attend the American School of Campinas in SaõPaulo for her senior year. Our missionary colleagues, Tom and Midge Foley, graciously agreed to have Shelley live with them and their family. This was partly to be near her Christian friends she had come to know from camp, and, I think, partly to be away from the negative influences of her old acquaintances in Recife.

In January, 1973, we had our first two-day camp near Recife with the young people of our group. Thirty-three attended and God blessed Beto and Cilas in the leadership of the program, which had its high point in the small group discussions. After this, we took Shelley back to Campinas and spent a few days' vacation there. Four from our Recife group had come with us and they, with Linda, attended a youth camp down south and they all returned to Recife by bus. Frank then drove to Brasília to take part in a Consultation between the Presbyterian Church, U. S., and the Presbyterian Church of Brazil. Tim and I took the train from Campinas to Brasĺlia, which was a unique experience. From there, the three of us returned home, completing over 4000 miles safely.

Everyone knows that water is essential to life, and that was true, of course, where we lived. In Recife, water pressure was good at night, with low demands, but weak during the day when demands were high. All the houses had water tanks (*caixa d' agua*) up high. The water would fill a cistern at night, and we would pump it into the *caixa* when needed. Shortly after moving to this house on the beach, the pump broke and we informed the landlord. He assured us he would have it fixed, but in the meantime, suggested we use a hose from the highrise next door, which he also owned, by telling their maid when we needed it to be turned on. It looked really strange to see this hose from the second floor of an apartment building extended to the house next door. We felt we could put up with this inconvenience for a week or two while the pump was repaired.

However, this situation continued for the next six months until we left to return to the States. Even in a modern city of over a million people, there were some things that kept us well aware we were still living in Brazil.

We were privileged to have Hal Merwald come from Campinas to hold a training retreat for the counselors, who would lead another three-day camp over Easter. He was a specialist working with youth under Young Life. Thirty-seven attended this camp and it was a joy to see such enthusiasm for the Lord's work. On the heels of that camp, the First Music Festival was held in our home with 75 young people filling every inch of space. There were original numbers on guitar and by voice. Some of these were included on song sheets used on the weekends.

Shelley graduated from High School, and I took the bus to Campinas to attend her graduation. There were two types of buses, and one was the Deluxe. I believe there were only 16 seats which reclined and had a foot rest. I'm not sure how many hours it took, but it was really a more comfortable trip than one by car. Shelley played her guitar and sang, "Morning has Broken" for graduation and it was so lovely. I was thankful to be with her and for us to have the trip home together.

On June 29th, 1973, Cilas and Tontonha were married in the interior of Brazil where she grew up. They never had enjoyed electricity out there, but they both wanted the ceremony recorded. So Cilas held a tape recorder during the ceremony. Frank married them, and also provided the music. They had been married the day before in a Civil Ceremony. I believe it was necessary to go the last few miles on donkey-back, so I decided not to go, but the family was represented. Cilas and Tontonha had met at Iracy's wedding four years earlier.

Two weeks after this happy occasion, we left for the States for a six-month furlough. Frank performed another wedding soon after our arrival. Our son Randy and Virginia Broadway, whom he had met in Chattanooga, were married in Biloxi,

Mississippi, on July 14. She was also one of six children, so there were a lot of siblings with whom to get acquainted. Ginny's Grandma and Grandpa Broadway had some trouble finding the Chapel on the Keesler Air Base and arrived a little late for the ceremony. Frank, being patient and understanding, asked Randy and Ginny to go through the ceremony again for her grandparents, which meant a lot to them.

The next month we went to Montreat for a meeting. Dr. Bell, Ruth Graham's father, died while we were there, and Frank played with two other men at the funeral service. The summer seemed to rush by with various reunions and obligations filling our days. Frank was busy with study groups at Central Church and made two trips to Washington, D.C. to visit associates in Christian Leadership.

As a family, we visited Terry and Ginny in Augusta, Maine, where she had a residency in Family Practice. I remember their unusual address: Three Mile Pond, South China, Maine. They had a huge St. Bernard who liked to keep cool at night wrapped around the commode. When I needed that space, he did not like to share. When we visited the capitol of Maine, Augusta, it was quite incongruous to see a jangada, the Brazilian fishing raft, in the center of the Capitol grounds. We found out that Augusta and Natal, capitol of Rio Grande do Norte, in northeast Brazil were sister cities.

And so our family had begun their habit of spreading out to far places: Terry in Maine, Dale in California and Randy in Tennessee. Shelley would be in Massachusetts as she enrolled that fall as a freshman at Gordon College north of Boston.

All six would be with us once more for Christmas before we left for Brazil on January 7. There was no way of foreseeing what was ahead of us in 1974. God knew the path we would take and also knew that He would reveal it to us, one step at a time, so we would not be overwhelmed by the enormity of the changes.

Oh may all who come behind us find us faithful
May the fire of our devotion light their way
May the footprints that we leave
Lead them to believe
And the lives we live inspire them to obey

Oh may all who come behind us find us faithful.

Informal family photo at Randall's wedding

Recife to Pittsfield 1974

Upon our return, we found ourselves being requested to consider a field outside of the Northeast Brazil, where we had served for 16 years. Our Mission was making a concerted effort to place personnel near the building of the Trans-Amazon Highway. It was not so much the fact of being asked to move, but it would mean leaving a work that was beginning to blossom and where our gifts were being used in a special way. We had spoken so often during our time in the States that God wanted us to be Flexible, Available, and Vulnerable, and now He wanted us to live this out every day. In April, we still did not know where we would be moving, but we were praying constantly that God would guide us to the right place.

Things progressed to the point that doors seemed to be closing for our continued stay in Brazil. It was a most heart-wrenching decision and one accompanied by prayer and many tears. It was comforting to know that the Christian Leadership Group under Sr. Torquato's leadership would continue. Jule Spach had helped to establish this group based on the model of the Prayer Breakfast Movement in Washington, D.C. and Brasília. Cilas and Tontonha were given faith to carry on with the youth work in Boa Viagem, trusting the Lord for their support. We said goodbye to our colleagues and many Brazilian friends in July, completing our eighth move since we had first come to Recife, eight years before.

To add to the trauma of leaving our beloved Brazil, our trip home came very close to being our last on this earth, which was not in the Lord's plan, I'm happy to say. Our 707 was coming in for a landing in Caracas, Venezuela, and at the last minute the plane pulled out of the descent with a powerful thrust upward. No word from the pilot, but those of us on the right side of the plane looked down to see heavy machinery on the runway on which we were to have landed. Still without a word to the passengers, he circled around and landed on the adjacent runway without incident. We were thankful for this deliverance, not only for ourselves, but for all those on board.

We again came home to Chattanooga, but this time without knowing our future plans. No one ever knows the future, but usually, we have a plan in mind. There was much correspondence and many conversations during the next few months, and in October we went on a leave of absence. With further considerations, it seemed best to offer our resignation to the division of International Missions of the Presbyterian Church in the United States.

Frank had been sending out résumés to many parts of the country, wanting to find the best place for us in the States. We were house sitting part of the time, and moving in with friends a week at a time. All this time, there didn't seem to be an opening for us. There was a church in Newark, New Jersey, which was looking for a bilingual pastor for a Portuguese congregation. This seemed to be a perfect match, and Frank went to candidate there. Then we waited and waited, with no answer.

In the meantime, he had also been approached by a church in Pittsfield, Massachusetts. When the opening in Newark seemed quite positive, we informed the people in Pittsfield. After about a month, we contacted the Newark church and found out they had called a man from Portugal. Next, Frank phoned Grace Church, Congregational, in Pittsfield, telling them of his availability. That very night, (I was told years later) the session was to have voted on another candidate, but without total agreement. Frank was then asked to visit the church and preach the next Sunday. When the session voted to call us, it was by a unanimous vote, and we understood what the Lord's plan was for us and where we were to go next.

Before we made the move to New England, we had the joy of welcoming our first grandson, Jason Randall Soules, born to Randy and Ginny on October 1, 1974.

We left Chattanooga the day before Thanksgiving, arriving in Pittsfield, MA, on the holiday, truly giving thanks for God's leading and His protection. Snow fell that night, and Tim was the first to go outdoors and write on the snow-covered windshield. He was an excited young boy, having seen so little snow before.

Starting life in Pittsfield, we were graciously received by the people of our new church and made to feel at home from the beginning. This church was under the Conservative Congregational Christian Conference, a fairly new denomination. Waiting had been hard, but we saw many pieces fit together. We rejoiced that we would be near most of our children, as well as Mom Soules and Frank's brothers. We were expectant to see how the Lord would use us in this new assignment in a traditionally liberal part of the country.

Grace Church Congregational 1974-1980

Our first home in Pittsfield was a rented one. This had been secured by the elders and was ready for us to move into. The people of the congregation were very generous in helping us to secure furniture – some new, some used and some borrowed. We moved in as winter was getting into full swing. The New Englanders said it was a mild winter. Being transported from the tropics to Northeastern USA, we began to doubt that this indeed could be true.

I was having coffee with a neighbor one morning in March, and she casually mentioned that it was unfortunate that we only had a six-month lease. We had assumed we had a year's lease, so this was a bit shocking. The men at the church had simply neglected to inform us of the fact. We began a frantic search for another house. We hoped to be able to buy, but it was not the best time of the year to be looking. However, we were led to an old house that had a lot of charm, (i.e., many nooks and crannies) and an affordable price. It needed work on the roof, and a lot of cosmetic improvements on the inside, but we made an offer, which was accepted, and we moved into our own home in February, 1975.

The house was situated on a State Highway, which meant the snow plows came early and often. This also meant we could clear off our driveway, and immediately have it covered with new snow from the plows. The plus side of winter was the beauty of everything right after a snow fall. In the summer, we had the privilege of seeing many hikers pass by our house. We were living on a portion of the Appalachian Trail. Frank and Tim planned to do a little hiking themselves on the Trail, and it was planned for weeks. They finally started out and were gone 5 days. It took me only an hour and a half driving time to pick them up at the end of their adventure. It had rained most of those days, but there was a real bonding between the two of them which meant a great deal from then on.

Linda started college early, attending Berkshire Christian College and at the same time getting credit for her senior year at Pittsfield High. In 1976 she was at Barrington College in Rhode Island for her sophomore year. She liked sports and played on the volleyball team. Shelley continued her studies at Gordon College and played on the Varsity volleyball team. After two years, she transferred to the University of Massachusetts so she could major in Early Childhood Education. Tim was enjoying the excellent electronics course at Taconic High and taking classes for extra credit. Terry and Ginny had moved to Atlanta and loved it. Dale graduated from New College of California in San Francisco. He continued working in the college library after graduation. He was also enjoying being in the music group called "Other Music." Randy was proving his ability in carpentry, which was evident by his winning the State Apprentice Carpenter's contest.

That summer of '76, we heard of a Student World Week in a nearby conference center called Hephzibah Heights. What attracted our attention initially was the speaker who was Christy Wilson, the minister who had come to Norwich Corners to help with Communion more than 25 years before. We knew nothing about International Students, Inc., the organization sponsoring the week. We took some vacation days and discovered this group of international students, mostly studying in New York City, who were interested in learning more about Christ and the Bible. Those who ran the Week, in turn, discovered that Frank had a distinct gift with his trumpet, and also in sharing from the Bible.

~~~~~ Grace Church Congregational 1974-1980 ~~~~~

Christy Wilson – Hephzibah Heights

The next summer and the ones following, we were asked to participate as part of the staff for Student World Week. It was our pleasure to become good friends with the directors of Hephzibah Heights, John and Lois Ewald. Their friendship would mean so very much in the years to follow. We became more involved with the students and by 1980, we were asked to consider joining ISI, (International Students, Inc.).

Frank felt his place was at Grace Church and thought he would be there until retirement age. The Lord works in mysterious ways, however, and the attraction of using our gifts with these students began drawing us closer and closer to ISI. He continued to minister at Grace Church for a few more years. I was par-

John and Lois Ewald

ticularly impressed at the manner in which he prayed for the members of his church. Every name was on a list, and each had been specifically prayed for by the end of the week. I believe this was his habit the whole ten years he ministered at Grace.

The winter of 1977 was very cold, but we were becoming accustomed to living in New England. A severe storm hit in March, and a tree fell on our house. Frank was on his way home from church, and with the signals and city lights being out, it was more difficult. We were also without electricity at home. When the tree hit the roof, the sound was deafening, and it was quite traumatic to be alone with Tim in a dark house. Fortunately, it fell against a slanted portion of the roof, instead of on the flat section, and the damage was lessened. Frank arrived home soon after the tree fell.

That summer Randy and Ginny came north to supervise work on the new roof. He worked hard and had lots of able helpers. He also tore out the ceiling in the back bedroom. The owners had apparently not bothered to fix a recurring leak, but instead covered it with a new ceiling several times. When Randy finally got to the bottom (or top) of the trouble, he had a five-inch space above the existing wallpaper. His solution of adding a wide molding made a very attractive addition. It was so good to have the leak permanently fixed also. After the repairs were finished, we had the joy of grandparenting Jason for a week while his parents toured New England.

Inspired by the outside improvements, I wanted new wallpaper in many of the rooms. Frank didn't have time to do it, so I got "how-to" books out of the library and proceeded to strip wallpaper. With some help from friends, I replaced the paper in the dining room, two bedrooms and a bath. When we got to the living room, I needed help getting all the old paper off the walls. After stripping off five layers, we actually uncovered the scores of a World Series Game of many years before. This whole process improved the appearance inside, but one's work is never done as the owner of a house.

I was attending a Bible study class in January 1977, where we were asked to write a Psalm of Praise. This was new to me, but I made an effort and wrote the following:

Your world that you made is beautiful.
Praise the Lord
The sky shows your glory,
The heavens reflect your brilliance.
Praise the Lord.
Each one of us is an individual,
Like snowflakes—no two alike,
And yet each one of your creations
Is made in your image
Praise the Lord.
Your supply of blueprints is inexhaustible,
So that you can mix each quality into the
Personality that you want.
Praise the Lord

Forgive us Lord, for letting our free will, which you gave us, nullify the plans you have for us. It is up to us, to become the people that you pictured in the beginning. Help me, O Lord, to become your person, with all the potential for being your child which only you know.

Don Lundgren made an unforgettable contribution to our church in Pittsfield. He served for many years as minister of Missions and used his violin to enhance each service that was held. The expertise of Frank and Don on their respective instruments gave a remarkable blend of music which was honoring to the Lord. In addition to his theological degree, Don had also gone through medical school and was a practicing physician.

In the fall, Shelley taught 1st grade as her practice teaching requirement for graduation, and completed her course in 1978. Tim was doing a good job as a disc jockey for the school's FM station, and loved getting his learner's permit when he turned sixteen. A neighbor had a Volkswagen "Bug" which didn't run. He gave it to Tim who learned a lot getting it into working condition. It was a strange experience for me to have a new driver in the family. The older boys had all learned in Brazil and had obtained their licenses while living away from home. Linda returned to Brazil that year, taking a semester at the Universidade Católica in Recife. She continued by studying through correspondence courses after that.

Our first granddaughter, Athena, was born March 8, 1979 to Terrill (he now preferred to use his given name) and Ginny. Nathaniel Edward was born to Randy and Ginny, on December 4, and their family was increased to four. It was just a coincidence that both daughters-in-law were named Ginny. The Soules clan was growing.

In addition to being involved in the women's activities at church, I wanted to serve in the community as well. For nearly three years, I worked as a Home Health Aide under the Visiting Nurse Association of Pittsfield. They started me out working a couple of hours at each home, helping in any way necessary – grooming, cooking, and administering medications.

Then, after a few months, I was assigned to one lady – five hours a day, five days a week. She was a delightful person who had been bedridden for thirty-five years with rheumatoid arthritis. She never complained, and after I helped her with her bath, she always wanted her earrings to match her night gown. She could feed herself and poke the buttons on her remote, which was the extent of her capabilities. She always wanted me to read from the Living Bible and have a prayer with her before I left for the day. I helped her for about two and a half years until she had to go into a Nursing Home. 1981 was fast approaching and my days would be filled with wedding preparations.

The Year of the Weddings 1981

We made our first trip back to Brazil for Christmas, 1980, to participate in Linda and Allan's wedding. Tim had recently become engaged, so Carol Brunjes, his fiancée, accompanied him. Shelley came with us too. The Brazilians always celebrate Christmas with a big dinner on Christmas Eve. Linda had asked me to bring sage and other ingredients necessary to make the stuffing for the turkey. I couldn't find celery in Brazil, but *chu-chu*, (chayote) was a fairly good substitute. Frank and I went over to the Neves', Allan's parents' house, in the morning to prepare the stuffing. We discovered that Lita, his mom, had marinated the turkey all night, so it would have been "counter-productive" to bake it with the dressing.

As we would be putting off the baking until afternoon, we prepared the bread and set it aside on the counter. That afternoon, we returned to finish the preparation. Without really looking at the container, I dumped in the bread and started stirring in the butter, vegetables, etc. To my horror, when I glanced more carefully, I saw that the bread was covered with ants, and half of the ingredients were already mixed in. There was nothing to do but to make a smaller amount and bake it, without the "extra protein." Everyone loved the stuffing, as Linda had predicted, but it was a shame there wasn't more of it. The dinner was delicious and it was so good to have this time with Allan's family.

The wedding was on January third, at eight in the evening. My job was to press the dresses for the four of us. Linda's gown had the most material, but Shelley, Carol and I also had long dresses. There was no ironing board, so I set up a table with a cover. I wanted to be able to use a steam iron which Carol had brought from home, but the voltage was 220 in Recife. This necessitated a heavy transformer to cut the voltage in half. Of course, as this was summer in the Southern Hemisphere, the day was very hot. It took me three hours to complete the task, which might be why I remember it so vividly.

Linda informed us that most of the guests would not be there by 8:00 p.m., so she didn't want to walk down the aisle until 8:30. Even then there were guests who came in later. It took place in the Capunga Baptist Church of Recife. She had requested the "impossible" of her father; walk her down the aisle, play the processional, and perform the ceremony. This was accomplished by using a recording of the music. The photographer took his time after the ceremony, and we were all delayed in getting downstairs to the reception. The caterers were beginning to put things away when Linda came down with all of us. She promptly took charge and the wedding party was able to join the others for the rest of the reception. I was sad that some of the people whom I hadn't seen in many years had already left.

We enjoyed being back in Brazil and spent two more weeks visiting old acquaintances. Frank made a trip back to Crato and Várzea Alegre, renewing ties with many dear people we had left fifteen years before.

The next six months were filled with preparations for two more weddings to be held in our church in Pittsfield. I had been taking some tailoring classes and decided to attempt to make a going-away suit for Shelley. It looked wonderful on her, but after a few years it was put away. (I was surprised and delighted to discover that the Vogue Classic design had weathered the years, and her daughter wore it 25 years later when she was teaching school.)

Shelley married Dieter Schmidt on June 14, and on June 20 Tim and Carol Brunjes were married. Dieter was from Switzerland and was studying at Berkshire Christian College in Lenox, Massachusetts. They designed and built the arbor under which they said their vows. This gave it the appearance of a garden. The reception was held at Dieter's college, and it was very special to have his brother and mother present from Switzerland. Shelley even joined them in some Swiss yodeling. She had gotten photos and slides from Dieter's mother and, together with her own slides from Brazil, gave a lovely presentation of their growing-up years on different continents.

Tim was hoping Shelley's wedding date would be earlier in the month, but he also wanted his three brothers to stand up with him. Thus the dates were set six days apart and all the siblings were present except Linda. It was a beautiful wedding with many guests as Carol had grown up in Massachusetts. Her sister, sister-in-law and a college friend and Tim's three brothers made up the wedding party. They had chosen June 20 because it was the anniversary of Carol's parents' wedding. Frank had had the privilege of marrying four of his children, and the unusual opportunity to also perform the marriage ceremony for his mother. Both Tim and Dieter had two more years of college to finish, and their wives had already graduated and were able to work, helping with the financial responsibilities. Tim was taking Electrical Engineering at Union College in Schenectady, New York.

InterVarsity Christian Fellowship had been holding a Conference for International Students every three years at Christmas time for a number of years in Urbana, Illinois. It was decided in 1981, that they would hold a Summer Urbana at Williams College, in Williamstown, Mass. This was to commemorate the Haystack Prayer Meeting in 1806 where five students took cover from a rain storm under a large haystack and asked the Lord to show them how they could be used to reach the unsaved around the world. This Summer Urbana Conference was held in August, marking the 175th anniversary of that historic event. The missionary vision of those five men would start the push to "take the gospel" around the world. Many Christian leaders came to take part in this anniversary event. Among them were Elisabeth Elliot, Gordon MacDonald, Ralph Winter and Christy Wilson. Christy was now a professor at Gordon Conwell Theological Seminary where Shelley had studied for a year before her marriage. Frank had written John Kyle, of InterVarsity, saying he would be willing to help in any way he could. They needed a song leader, so Frank led all the music, using his gift of song leading as well as using his trumpet in such a distinctive way. It was an honor to be present for this truly historical Missionary event.

At the Haystack Monument from left, Betty Wilson, Frank and me, Steve Van Blarcom, Christy and Tom Downie

Our Last Years in Pittsfield 1981-84

We started thinking about downsizing in 1982, and decided to sell our house. This was finally accomplished, and we moved into a rented two-story dwelling. We had no idea how providential this would be in the near future.

With Shelley and Dieter living in Pittsfield, we had the privilege of seeing Andrea Michelle hours after she was born on July 20, 1983. They moved to Switzerland nine months later, but it was "fun while it lasted." On September 27, Hudson joined Athena and his parents, Terrill and Ginny, and we all fell in love with him.

Albanize, Allan's sister, wanted to come to the States and spend some time with us so she would get a better grasp of English. We went to pick her up at JFK airport in New York. We waited an unusually long time and all the passengers had seemingly come through customs. The US was experiencing a lot of young girls entering the States illegally in those days as "au pairs," and customs officials were overly cautious checking them through. When she finally reached us, she said they had read the letters she was bringing to people in this country and had gone through her luggage quite thoroughly. We were all ready for some coffee, so we went into a coffee shop in the airport. This was providential, as she was soon approached by a customs person, and asked to identify herself. She was then handed her passport and her money in an envelope, which she had left behind in the confusion with the customs officers. We were so thankful we had not left the airport immediately.

Soon after Alby (her nickname) came to live with us, she wanted to fulfill a dream of visiting Disney World. I agreed to accompany her, and we flew to Florida where I rented a car. Our visit coincided with the week in 1983 that the shuttle, Challenger 7 was to be launched. This was quite significant in that Sally Ride was the first American woman to be on a space shuttle. A friend who had been in our church in Pittsfield had connections and was able to get me a gate pass to witness the launch. We were both excited about this opportunity, but a lot was involved. We had to check out of the hotel at 3:00 a.m. and buy a small cooler and some food as we had been informed there was no food on the base. Thus prepared, I drove to the base at Cape Canaveral, arriving before dawn. I think the launch was scheduled for 7:30 and it was delayed some. What a thrilling experience to watch it in person. Of course, we were across the water, but the noise and reality of it was very memorable.

When all the excitement died down, and we had eaten, I realized I was completely blocked in by cars on all sides. It was imperative that I return the car to the rental office at the airport, over an hour away, before boarding the plane. A few cars left, but I was still blocked. I explained my situation and some strong men took pity on us and actually moved (manually) the one car that stood between me and "freedom." We made the flight but with very little time to spare.

So our six months saga began, having a very attractive twenty-year-old living with us, who soon had a following of young men from the church. In her sweet Brazilian manner, she would be very encouraging to each one. As I listened some to her phone conversations, I warned her not to be quite so forward with the boys. She assured me that they knew she didn't "mean" anything by it. I let her know that they very well might. She learned more of our customs, and also learned English quite well.

At the end of her stay one of the young men in the church returned from the Service. There was a very definite attraction between them, and before she left, Bill Sack promised to visit her in Brazil, which he did. Then Alby came back for a visit. Before long they were engaged and Frank married them in 1985. They are now living in Texas and raising their family of three sons.

Tim graduated from Union College in 1983, with the unique distinction of getting his Bachelor's and Master's degrees in Electrical Engineering the same day. He was elected into Eta Kappa Nu and Tau Beta Pi, the national honor fraternities of Electrical and Computer Engineering and Engineering, respectively. Dieter earned his Bachelor of Theology with an emphasis in Missions that same year. Even studying in English as his second language, he graduated Magna Cum Laude. His parents came for this auspicious occasion, the first time to America for his father.

Frank was privileged to go with a group of pastors and laymen to England in October, 1983. Luis Palau had invited him to participate in the final weeks of his "Mission to London" Crusade. Our connection with Luis Palau was through Grace Church in Pittsfield, where he had spoken.

International Students, Inc. 1984-86

By 1984, we had become convinced of God's call on us to work with international students under ISI. So Frank resigned from the pastorate at Grace Church and planned to work with staff in the Boston area after our orientation and internship. We would be leaving a secure position (according to some) and raising our support in a faith-based ministry.

We had many friends at Grace Church and in the city of Pittsfield. It was a sad time to leave them, and yet, it was exciting to know we were going where God was leading. Because we had been renting, it was a simple matter to put our belongings in storage, leaving us free to travel during our internship. First we needed to go to the headquarters of ISI in Colorado Springs and spend a few weeks. Then, it was Atlanta for two months.

Terrill convinced us that we needed a computer to handle the mailing list and letters we would be writing. This was 1984 and we knew nothing about computers. We were convinced of the wisdom of this, however, and bought an Epson. Oh, so long ago in capabilities and speed of a computer! Frank was good at writing, and he kept our supporters informed regularly. We were so thankful for their faithfulness. As our support base grew, I began to enter name after name in a data base and built up our mailing list. It was slow and the printer was an "antique" compared to today's standards. But it got us started, thanks to Terrill's urging. We were so green and untrained, that our first letter was printed out on our printer – all 200 copies – instead of having them copied downtown.

Tim and Carol were thrilled to welcome Jessica Ruth on October 13, 1984, and we were so thankful for her safe arrival.

On February 2, 1985, Catarina Soules Neves (Linda chose the Brazilian custom of using the mother's last name as well) became our first international granddaughter when Linda and Allan welcomed their little "Latin doll." We would have to wait until the proposed reunion in '86 to actually get to meet her.

After working in the South, we were asked to consider a nine months' internship in New York City, living at Hephzibah House. The Ewalds lived there during the school year, and we were glad that we would be with them during this time. There were other things to consider, however, and I really did want to get my furniture out of storage and get settled in our new home. Of course, that would have to wait if we were to live in NYC.

After praying about this, we felt that this exposure to the vast number of international students in New York would be excellent training for later on. So we moved into Hephzibah on the 5th floor – no elevator. This was a house open to Christian workers who needed temporary housing in the city. There were no meals provided. However, the Ewalds made provision for us to eat with them, which was most welcome. The kitchen was in the basement, so by necessity I was becoming more physically fit. Frank didn't want to disturb any of the residents, so every night he would go down to the kitchen to practice his trumpet.

We were settling into a routine as we met regularly with the international students at Hephzibah House. This was located on W. 75th St. just a block west of Central Park. It was close to bus and subway transportation, and after two months, we sold our car. It was such a hassle to move it from one side of the street to the other, and then back, every other day to comply with the cleaning of the streets.

Hannah Joy joined the Schmidt family on April 22, 1985, and was definitely a "Swiss Miss." Some dear friends of ours wanted us to be able to visit Shelley and Dieter in Switzerland that summer and graciously provided for the trip. Frank felt we should be saving for the family reunion which was planned for

July, 1986, so he offered to stay home, but urged me to go without him. I regretted the fact that he wasn't with me to enjoy the beauty of Switzerland and to welcome our new granddaughter, but I thoroughly enjoyed my first trip to Europe.

The attendance was growing at our Tuesday night suppers and Bible studies. Frank and I made a point of taking off one day a week and doing something together. We would go out to eat, visit a museum, or visit one of the sights in New York. Sometimes, we would just ride the Staten Island Ferry if it was a nice day.

In February, 1986, we celebrated our 40th anniversary by going to a Brazilian restaurant with the Ewalds. We had no way of knowing that would be the last time we would be going out on such a happy occasion.

Frank's Illness 1986

Since being in New York, Frank had joined the orchestra, made up mostly of Julliard students, at Calvary Baptist Church. They played once a month on a Sunday evening. One evening in February, however, was different. He told me on the way home that something was wrong; he had made all kinds of mistakes on his horn.

We called our good friend, Dr. Don Lundgren, and he advised Frank to get a CT scan. We went back to Pittsfield to have this done. On March 5, the doctor informed us of the presence of a brain tumor. Philippians 4:6, 7 came to mind. "Do not be anxious about anything, but in everything, by prayer and petition, with thanksgiving, present your requests to God. And the peace of God which transcends all understanding will guard your heart and your minds in Christ Jesus." We tried to think of this verse often, but it was not easy.

This was so difficult to understand, but we trusted God to help us and show us the way. It was difficult to call the children with the news, but I told them I was hoping and praying we would still be able to have our reunion in July. We felt it would be better to return to NYC where there would be excellent hospitals and doctors, and where I would have a home base. John and Audrey Downie took us back to the city.

Frank began to lose mobility in his right arm and hand. Dale arrived on Sunday, March 9, and it was very good to see him. With his help, I was able to send out about 300 "Prayer alert letters," so that our friends in many parts of the country would be aware of Frank's condition. On March 11, the three of us went to the Neurological Institute and met with Dr. Fetell, the oncologist.

After performing many of the same tests that had been done in Pittsfield, the doctor felt Frank should be admitted to the hospital. They did an MRI to better determine the nature and location of the tumor. The doctor told me that the MRI machine was one of only two in the country! Dr. Paul Lauterbur had developed this machine in his basement in Ohio. By the time he and a Briton won the Nobel Prize for their discovery in 2003, more than 60 million scans were being performed worldwide every year.

Tim arrived on the 13th and it was a great comfort to me to have two of my sons with me at this very difficult time. Dr. Housepian was Frank's surgeon and always took time to explain procedures and his progress. He wanted us to understand about the experimental drug Interferon if the tumor proved to be malignant. Frank signed papers for permission for an operation and also for the use of Interferon. His writing was deteriorating rapidly. One of the last things he signed was an endorsement on a check for the final payment for a property in Venice, California. He had to push the paper with his left hand so he could make the letters. He had inherited this house many years before, along with his brothers and two cousins. I was thankful to be able to distribute the last payment to each of the parties involved. We had prayer around his bed before leaving for the night.

As is common with Frank's kind of brain tumor, he suffered several seizures, some quite severe. His surgery was scheduled for 8:30 a.m. Monday, March 17th. The three of us arrived early to see him before he went into surgery, and all the other kids had talked to him on the phone. I would always read a portion of the Bible with him which he seemed to appreciate. Isaiah 46:4 was one of the verses. "Even to your old age and gray hairs, I am he; I am he who will sustain you. I have made you; I will sustain you and I will rescue you." We were all a bit teary-eyed as we walked him to the elevator. When we returned in the afternoon, the doctor came to the waiting room to tell us that the tumor was malignant, but he felt he had gotten it all. Tim had to go home that evening to be with Carol, whose Dad was to have his arm amputated the following Wednesday. It was so hard for Tim and Carol to face such traumatic situations with both of their fathers.

A new development after surgery was Frank's inability to move his right leg. He also had difficulty speaking. By the time Dale left on March 21st, there was little improvement in his dad's leg movement, but the doctors said they would start some physical therapy the next week.

I had an answering machine in my room at Hephzibah, and there were many messages when we arrived home. I taped them so I could take them to the hospital when Frank was more alert to listen to them. I also wanted his friends to know how he was progressing each day, so I changed the outgoing message daily. Even a 30-second update kept them informed. It was comforting to know so many of our friends were praying for Frank and me. It was only natural that I often wondered what the future might hold. But I knew that people were not only praying for Frank, but for me as well – that I would be given strength every day. I did feel well most of the time, but fatigue was more apparent as the weeks went by.

On Palm Sunday, Pastor Hubbard at Calvary Baptist dedicated a presentation of the Messiah to Frank. He was to have played three solos that day, but they were taken over by another trumpeter.

Every day I would make the subway trip to the Columbia Presbyterian Hospital on 148th Street. John Ewald or someone from the House would come to go home with me so I wouldn't travel alone after dark. Each day Frank was more lethargic, and he was unable to make himself understood very well. Another CT scan revealed the presence of a cyst and some blocked veins, explaining his lack of response. Dr. Housepian felt a second surgery was necessary. It took place on the 26th. John Eaves, our ISI Regional Director in Boston, didn't want me to be alone that day, so he graciously came to be with me. We were able to see Frank twice in ICU, and then John and I went out to dinner. It was so helpful and such a comfort to have him there all day. I had lots of questions about ISI and what my future might hold. Of course, we didn't have all the answers at that time, but it was good to have someone to talk to about possibilities.

The doctor decided Frank needed a private room, so for the second time, we had privacy and were only charged for a semi-private, which was covered by our insurance. The next few days the medical staff tried to regulate his diet and medication, because he wasn't responding too well. By April, physical therapy began and was scheduled for six weeks. Kevin was the therapist in charge and they had a good rapport. Of course, Frank had to stay in the hospital for the therapy, because it would have been impossible for him to be transported back and forth.

Terrill came on April 4th and Frank was pleased to see him. The next day Randall came, which was special for them to be there together. They gave me such a boost by their support. It wasn't easy, day after day, seeing so little progress. When we left the hospital, they wanted to have a good Brazilian meal, so we went to the same restaurant where Frank and I had celebrated our anniversary. It was hard to believe that less than six weeks had passed since that special day. The boys loved the meal, and it brought back many happy memories. I hated to think about them leaving the next day.

Hundreds of friends were joining me in praying for Frank's healing, and it was hard to accept the fact that it might not work out that way. When one prays for God to answer, the answer is not always "Yes," but it is always right.

Just before Frank's illness, we had started a new class for internationals called Master Life. Frank and Marion Paxton were going to team teach. It now fell on her shoulders, and she did an admirable job continuing what had just begun. In NYC we knew several Philippine nurses whom we had met at Calvary Baptist. These dear ladies came every so often to stay with Frank and give me a little time off, which was much appreciated.

I felt it was important to get word to all those on our mailing list, which now had more than 600 names. I was able to get a letter written and sent off by April 10 – a huge job.

Radiation therapy began, but often the scheduling conflicted with his physical therapy, which was frustrating to both of us. I felt so weak myself, but I believed that God would help me to understand whatever was to happen. I often said, "I can't ask 'Why,' because there wouldn't be any answer."

The Sack family came from Pittsfield, and I was overwhelmed by their kindness of taking a whole day to come spend just a short time with Frank, which was all he could tolerate. Don and Lissa Lundgren came more than once, as did the Crawfords. Shelley's close friend, Mary Ellen Bricker came with her husband and sang some hymns which pleased Frank. Tom Downie made the trip from Washington, D.C., and Dick Burr also took time to visit. He ministered to me as well, helping me to have some perspective in facing the future. Tom and Charlene Bridgman came all the way from Vermont so Frank could see their new son, Ian. John and Lois exhibited an "open heart" and "open home" policy, and they always found room for any of my family to stay at Hephzibah House. There were many others who dropped by to say hello to Frank and to wish him well.

It was nearly a month after his first surgery that phlebitis developed and he had a blood clot in his right leg. This meant complete bed rest with no physical therapy for two weeks. Heparin was started by IV. Radiation was continued, and they had to transport him with the IV bottle on a pole. He was talking better, but one day he asked, in agony, "Why does this have to be happening to me? But God's will be done."

It meant a great deal to Frank to have his brother Paul bring his Mom to visit, and she was glad to find him speaking quite well by then.

I needed to be strong, but it was hard not to be able to lean on Frank's strength as I had always done. John Ewald was willing to share his wisdom with me, and we often talked about what I was going through. I made a collage of family photos in a frame, trying to keep Frank aware that his far-flung children were with him in spirit. They called often, and they were all very concerned. Our many friends phoned or sent cards, often with gifts, to express their love to one who meant the world to them.

His speech began to decline once more due to build-up of fluid in the cyst. However, he would volunteer to pray occasionally at meal times. It was a joyful occasion when Frank called me on the phone on April 27th. He was feeling some better. His physical therapy had begun again, but he hadn't been taken off Heparin.

For the first time in two months, I attended a Master Life study. They were all happy to see me and clapped when I came in. Marion was doing an admirable job keeping the group going. After class, some of us went to supper and then to the Empire State Building. It was a lovely night and a beautiful view. It was the first time since Frank went to the hospital that I had gone out, and it was a therapeutic change. I had those "Wednesdays" with Frank to remember and be thankful for.

One might say that Frank was the ideal patient. He was usually cheerful and accepting of all the many things he had to endure. The nursing staff was great, and the doctors monitored his progress closely. His leg was gaining strength, and Kevin continued to give him good physical therapy sessions.

I was already at the hospital the morning Tim called to tell us that Aaron Timothy was born on May 5th. We were delighted, and I put the announcement on our door telling everyone about our new grandchild – number 9.

No matter when I returned to Hephzibah House, supper was waiting and usually I could stop by John and Lois' room to give them a report and have a prayer with them.

Frank's Illness 1986

Frank had a few more seizures and Dr. Housepian had to drain the cyst once more. He was gaining a bit more strength in his leg, and we were hoping he could improve enough for him to be transferred to the 8th floor for rehabilitation. On Mother's Day, I was pleased and surprised to get a lovely card from Frank. He had asked one of the nurses to buy it, and he had laboriously written a wonderful message. It was so very sweet of him to think of doing this. One night I brought turkey sandwiches for both of us, and that was a treat to be able to have a meal together. I was tired of eating alone, and I'm sure he was tired of hospital food.

It was hard to face reality, but I wrote in my journal that night, "Oh, God, I pray you will give Frank quality time for the months granted to him. I pray that we may be given grace and peace to accept whatever happens. It is so difficult to think of the realities ahead of us. I ask for strength and wisdom through the months ahead. I am so thankful for the 40 wonderful years we have shared. Our love for each other is precious."

Frank's smile when I entered his room was reward enough each day to tell me how important my visits were to him. He encouraged me to go to a concert in which Marcus Hulse was playing. He was the trumpeter who took Frank's place in the Messiah. I realized how hard it was for Frank to think of this important part of his life being wrenched away, not knowing if he would ever get it back.

He had a leg brace made from a mold of his foot and back of his leg. This was to give him more support when walking. His progress would be good in some areas and regressive in others. When he was transferred to the 8th Floor Rehab. on May 22nd, I began to wonder if he really would be able to be at the reunion, or if we would go ahead with it in Massachusetts if he was in New York City. So many questions!! Very few answers!

He was in a much more relaxed environment then, got around by himself in the wheelchair and ate in the sunroom.

He got dressed every day – no longer in hospital attire, but in sweats and a shirt. They kept him busy during the day, so my visits were limited to 5-8:00 p.m.

At the end of May, I was able to make a 4-day trip to Massachusetts. I spent two days in Pittsfield, and then on to Boston, where I talked with John Eaves about my situation and the need to move into an apartment. It wouldn't have been complete without seeing little Aaron, Jessica, and Tim and Carol in Ipswich. What cute babies and a delight to be able to visit them.

Linda came from Brazil on May 31st with baby Catarina and Lita, Allan's mother. Frank was delighted to see the baby and also to see Linda after so many months. Linda had arranged to have the baby stay in Massachusetts with our dear friends, the Lundgrens, so she came back to be of help to me and to visit more with Dad. I was able to find an apartment on Riverside Drive close to the hospital, which seemed to be the answer to a way to keep Frank at home, which I was hoping for. Linda and I had a lot of work to clean up the place and to buy the necessities to set up housekeeping. In hindsight, I think it was probably visionary and wishful thinking to prepare an apartment for Frank. Linda was noticing more change in Frank than I was because it had been so gradual. The enjoyment of eating in the sunroom was negated by many of the patients smoking after eating. This certainly did not enhance the ambiance.

Sue Fisher came to see Frank and took Linda and me out to dinner. It was the first time we had seen her since her visit in Recife.

Frank's speech was getting harder to understand, and the doctors weren't sure why. Dr. Housepian ordered another CT scan. The results were discouraging, to say the least. The tumor had returned and was larger than the first time, even after all the Cobalt radiation. To add to this frustration, we had to compete with Jamaican TV and Spanish TV on either side of us in the room. It was less than an ideal climate to try to talk and read the Bible.

Frank's Illness 1986

Tim took a week off and came to help me move. I had to have a few pieces of furniture brought from Pittsfield – just the bare essentials. John Downie made two trips to Riverside Drive, moving everything I had accumulated at Hephzibah. I was quite overcome when I finally left my room at Hephzibah alone, having moved in eight months earlier with Frank and with great expectations for the future. Now the future meant tomorrow or next week.

We made many trips to JFK airport – first to greet Shelley with the two girls, then Dieter who came a week later. Allan came after that, and the subway trips were always lengthy. Frank was able to leave the hospital for an overnight on June 28th. He hadn't realized it was for only one night and was very disappointed when he had to return to the hospital. His next visit to the apartment was on the 4th of July. We all enjoyed watching the parade of the "Tall Ships" from many countries. Frank especially loved seeing the three little granddaughters interact in two, and sometimes three languages. There was a big mix-up in getting transportation back to the hospital. The pre-arranged taxi never came, and finally I got an ambulance at 11:00 p.m. By then, he was exhausted and had missed his 9:00 p.m. medication.

By July 7th he was in a decline, not responding at all. They started IV's, and by evening he was semi-conscious and had been moved to the Neurological floor. On the 9th, an alert nurse noticed his pupils were dilated. Manitol was started to reduce pressure in the brain. I stayed overnight in the hospital with Linda. The next day he was responding, and enjoyed visits from his mom and from the Crawfords. But two days later, when Dieter flew in, Frank was in a coma once more and unable to respond. This one lasted about two days, and then, once more he started to show improvement. Dieter was able to talk with him then, as well as Tim and Carol. Frank was delighted to see little Aaron for the first time.

Although Frank was unable to return to the apartment, it gave lots of floor space for mattresses for 11 of us on July 14. With the reunion only four days away, I was resigned to going just for the weekend, and spending the rest of the time with Frank at the hospital. When I mentioned this, he would begin to cry.

Family Reunion
July, 1986

I believe a phone conversation I had with Steve Crowe was a turning point in my thinking. He explained what it had meant to his father to have his four boys with him before he died. From that moment on, I was determined that Frank would be with us at the reunion – after all, he was the father of this tribe. My mindset went from resignation to determination, and whether by ambulance, helicopter or van, he would be with us. Once again John Downie came, and provided the means to take Frank to Lenox, Massachusetts, right next to Pittsfiield. There were many goodbyes from the doctors and nurses and numerous instructions for me concerning care and medication. Frank had been at that same address for four months and a week. I was grateful that Tim had come once again to help me with this move.

We made the trip without incident, only stopping twice on the way. When we finally pulled into the DeVos farm about 7:30 p.m., many of the children were there to greet Frank. I felt it was truly a mir-

The DeVos Farm

acle, considering his condition only a week before. Within the hour Randy, Shelley, and Linda all arrived with their respective families completing the final number. It was the culmination of planning which had started 18 months beforehand. I had not thought about the need for a hospital bed and a wheelchair, but Chris Petell and Carol had arranged those. And Frank had four strong boys to move him wherever he needed to be.

No gathering of this magnitude could take place without a photographer. Terrill had his video camera, also. Before we finished the photo-shoot on the 19th, Paul and his mom arrived and they were included.

That week went by so fast; filled with happy laughter, games, eating outdoors, children playing in the barn, and a cow getting loose. We even went to Bonanza for dinner as a group when someone stayed with Frank. The most memorable thing was Frank's wide smile and his joy of being with his family. His words were few and far between, but that didn't matter.

Frank, July 19, 1986

Little Aaron was two months and Jason, the oldest, was almost 12 years old. They all had a grand time of getting acquainted or reacquainted. All those who could, wrote in our memory book, and it was evident the week was meaningful as well as fun for each one. We shared in the cooking, and many friends from church brought meals or some snacks. Millie DeVos and her son had unselfishly given over her 10-room house to us, which was truly wonderful. I got very little sleep, since I got up every two hours to give Frank his medications, but my adrenalin kicked in every morning, and I loved every minute of

Family Reunion July 1986

The Whole family 1986: from left, front row, Ginny with Hudson, Catarina, Nathaniel, Andrea, Ardy and Frank, Carol with Aaron, Jason, Terrill, Athena and Linda; back row, Dale, Janet Tallman, Randall, Ginny, Shelley with Hannah, Dieter, Baird with Jessica, and Allan.

it. How thankful I was that he never again lapsed into a coma, and that he weathered the excitement of the reunion very well.

It was very emotional to see each family leave and say goodbye to their dad. It was obvious he could not return to NYC, and decisions had to be made. The Crawfords graciously offered us a place to stay for the immediate future, turning their living room into a hospital room of sorts. Linda and Catarina were able to be with me for a couple of weeks, staying with our friends, Tom and Jean Porter, and I was always in touch with the other children.

After a few weeks, it seemed wise to find our own place in Pittsfield, which would mean leaving the apartment in New York City. This necessitated my being away for about a week, so with a heavy heart I put Frank into a Nursing Home temporarily. He couldn't talk much, but I knew he was very unhappy with this arrangement. A friend wrote to me later about Frank's being in the Nursing Home. She said that the wife of a patient there said that Frank held out his hand to her and held it for several minutes. His loving, caring look made a profound impression on her. Even without speaking, he always seemed to convey Christ's love.

Once again, my furniture needed to be moved, and some men from our church in Pittsfield helped in this task. The landlady in New York City was not the least bit understanding and would not return my deposit because the time was two weeks shy of the notice she required.

Frank left the Nursing Home, and I brought him home to our apartment. Dr. Perera, a friend in the church, took over Frank's care, and my sister, Janet, offered to come and help me for two weeks. This was not only appreciated because of her nursing skills, but also for her willingness to come and give me support and encouragement. She left on September 20th, and the days were pretty much of a blur from then on.

I called Dr. Perera on the night of September 28th telling him that Frank's breathing was very labored and he was not responding. He came right over, but dear Frank had passed from this life of pain and sorrow to his eternal home where there were no tears, and where he met his Savior whom he had served all his life. Dick stayed with me and called the Funeral Home, and I called all the children. Then he insisted on taking me to his home where his dear wife, Eve, welcomed me and comforted me.

The funeral service on October 2, 1986 was held at Grace Church Congregational where Frank had served for 10 years. It was a testimony to a life well lived, and it was evident that Frank and I had many wonderful friends. They came from Colorado, New York, Boston, and of course, from the surrounding area. During the course of the years at Grace Church, Frank had discipled several young men. Some went into the ministry, but all of them were keeping Christ as the head of their homes.

Let me quote from letters we received from two of these young men. "The one lesson you taught me by your example was submission. You truly have taught me what it means to have a surrendered submissive spirit. My heart-felt thanks to you Frank." And Tom Bridgman, who would later succeed him as pastor of Grace Church, wrote me after Frank died, "Ardy, I don't know if you realize just how much impact Frank had on my life and my preparation for the ministry. I am always running into situations where I ask myself, 'What would Frank do in this case?' I want you to know that I have decided to adopt the same verse of scripture that Frank did as my life verse. Philippians 1:20."

Most of these men came back and served as pall bearers at Frank's funeral. Tim had come to help me make arrangements. We had found a slip of paper in Frank's Bible where he had written down the names of men he wanted to assist in the funeral. He also wrote the scriptures and songs he wanted. He wanted joy to be more evident than sadness. What made this so remarkable was that he had dated this in 1981, five years before his death. He had made some recent changes in his shaky handwriting, but he wanted to be prepared, the same way he had lived his whole life.

Frank laid to rest in Pittsfield, Massachusetts

His body was laid to rest in the Pittsfield Cemetery. Our four boys were with me, but the girls had already returned to Brazil and Switzerland by then. Tim and I designed the tombstone. I wanted to include the reference of Frank's life verse under his name. Philippians 1:20 certainly was a picture of his life. "I eagerly expect and hope that I will in no way be ashamed, but will have sufficient courage so that now as always Christ will be exalted in my body, whether by life or by death."

This story started out to be the story of my life, but my life would have been so very different without Frank, so this last chapter is dedicated to him and to the family as well.

Just as I have had to walk by faith and not by sight many times in my life, I will continue to do so, trusting the Lord to guide and direct my path. I have no doubt that this relationship will be blessed if I rest in God's faithfulness, and not my own ability. This will be a new chapter, with different characters, but Frank would have wanted me to continue working with the internationals as long as possible, and that is what I plan to do.

How very special to have my family, even though scattered geographically, but very near in spirit. I have been truly blessed.

After all our hopes and dreams have come and gone and our children sift through all we've left behind
May the clues that they discover and the memories they uncover
Become the light that leads them to the road we each must find.

Part Two

International Students, Inc.

This new chapter in my life began as I worked through grief and countless memories. In January, 1987 I wrote a letter marking "passages" for 1986. "As I reflect on this year full of passages, I know that it was only possible to arrive at this new stage in my life because of the way the Lord has helped me …. I can look forward to yet more creative ways in which God will show me that He cares."

The first task in October was to vacate the little apartment in Pittsfield we had been in less than a month. Once again, furniture was put in storage, and I had to make decisions regarding my future and a different life. Next it was necessary to determine where my area of service would be if I continued with ISI. I felt this was the ministry in which to be involved, but I needed direction. I spent nearly three weeks with personnel at headquarters in Colorado Springs and was encouraged to use the training I had already received and be assigned to work in connection with a university.

Personally, I didn't want to face winters living alone in New England, so that pointed me in the direction of the South. In February before Frank took ill we had both participated in a seminar at the Congress '86 in Boston, sharing our vision for reaching out to internationals. This was sponsored by the Evangelical Association of New England (EANE). At that time, it seemed our future ministry was to be in the Boston area. But now all indications pointed to returning to the South where we had lived for many years. God had it all planned out and gave me the will and the ability to fit into this new life.

Our organization already had staff working in Virginia, North and South Carolina, Georgia, and Knoxville, Tennessee, as well as other southern centers. My ties were in Chattanooga, however, with one son there and many friends from our years spent in that city. The policy of ISI was to avoid sending staff where they did not have staff already working in the local university. We prayed about my situation and it was decided that they would approve my move to Chattanooga. I would begin making contacts at the University of Tennessee at Chattanooga (UTC.) I joined First Presbyterian Church which had been a partner with us all our years in Brazil.

All my belongings were in Massachusetts, and I had to find a place to live. I flew to Atlanta and Bob Culver brought me to Chattanooga. I had three days to locate a dwelling that would be suitable. Renting was always an option if no suitable place was found to buy. A friend of mine who was in Real Estate showed me a condo in an ideal location. I asked if she had others available and she said, "Yes, but they are more expensive." So I didn't look any further.

This first condo had two floors, but it was an ideal size. I offered the seller $4000.00 less than the asking price, and he accepted within the hour. I was able to use the money we got from the Venice property for a down payment. It was empty, so I could move right in. This was all new to me, but God gave direction and it seemed to be the perfect next step.

Part Two: International Students, Inc.

The next day, I returned to Massachusetts and the whole transaction was handled by Fed-Ex. It was December and I had many items of furniture to dispose of. Tag sales are usually held in the spring, but putting all the items in Margaret Barbour's two-car garage and advertising a "winter sale" seemed to do the trick. What I didn't sell or give away I took to Chattanooga. The moving van pulled up on Bacon Trail and unloaded my belongings, and by the end of January I was settled in. I soon welcomed my two sisters, Janet and Nayda, as my first visitors in my new home.

I believe the combination of a move, a new residence and new responsibilities helped me a great deal with the very real grief of losing my life partner. I knew many people were praying for me, writing me and sharing in the financial end of my ministry. I was truly upheld and encouraged. It's not that I no longer missed Frank, because I did, but knowing God's hand was in this transition made it easier to accept. Two things seemed to trigger waves of sorrow for me at first. Obviously, every time I heard a trumpet for a long time, especially one playing songs Frank had played, unleashed the wells of water in my eyes. I had picked out shirts and ties for Frank for years, and now passing a men's store was difficult, knowing I would no longer be shopping for those items.

We had not owned a car for over a year, so I was faced with this purchase as well. I was thankful for good advise and, not incidentally, the ability to drive confidently. I studied the Motor Vehicle booklet and took my written test. With four mistakes I would not have passed. I had three – all having to do with DUI's and permissible alcohol levels. I had not bothered to read that section, thinking it did not apply to me.

In May, 1987, I was invited to speak at a Pastor's Wife's Retreat in New York City. It was an awesome challenge, but the Lord helped me to make it meaningful to those attending.

In the summer of 1988, I was asked to return to Hephzibah Heights to function as registrar for the many conferences held

Nayda and Janet came from California by train

there. This was approved by my superiors at ISI and so I was to be back in Massachusetts for an extended period. I knew I would need my own transportation, but I was not used to driving long distances. Making stops with friends along the way and having a reliable car all coincided to give me a good trip.

It was wonderful to see Baird and Carol and the grandchildren again. (Tim had started using his middle name.) It was wonderful to see many old friends at Hephzibah, both colleagues and internationals. The cooling breezes in the Berkshires were a welcome relief from the hot summers down South. The speakers were inspirational and it was especially gratifying to be with John and Lois Ewald again. They spent the summers at the Heights instead of in New York City. Many people spoke of missing the golden tones of Frank's trumpet when he would waken the guests with a hymn or two in years gone by.

After leaving the Heights in July, I attended the Annual Meeting of the Conservative Congregational Christian Conference, The 4 Cs, in Houghton, New York and then flew to California to visit my sister and my son, Dale. Then I included a stop in Colorado for the triennial ISI conference, a first for me in my new capacity. I flew back to Massachusetts and once more I was driving south to arrive in time for the fall picnic in August.

PART TWO: International Students, Inc.

As I got settled in my condo, I began making contacts at UTC. Help from the Foreign Student Advisor, who was a Christian, was much appreciated. It wasn't until school started in the fall of 1988 that I was led to an opportunity to tutor English in the Special Services Department. This gave me openings for further conversations with the international students. Some of my ministry was getting local churches involved. I spoke in several and attended Mission Conferences at two of my supporting churches. When there were community celebrations where the students could participate, three or four of us would ask them to join us. These included Pops Concerts outdoors on Memorial Day and Labor Day. A picnic supper always added to the fun.

There was, as yet, no group at the church that was ministering to this strategic "mission field at our doorstep." A few individuals were seeing the opportunities and meeting some of the internationals. One time I was at the airport to meet a student coming from China. We ate at a restaurant before checking him into the dorm. I casually asked him if he wanted rice or potatoes. He looked very surprised saying, "I thought I wouldn't get any rice for four years." Such are the erroneous opinions about American customs. Needless to say, he was pleasantly surprised.

As an expansion of teaching English as a second language, I started a cooking class with several of the Japanese women. We would meet in one of their homes and bake something. The recipe would be printed with "new" English words on the bottom of the page. While the "cooking" was progressing, we would have our English lesson and end up enjoying the finished product. Most of these women were wives of Japanese men connected with the local Komatsu plant for large machinery.

When trips were planned during Spring Breaks, I often accompanied the students on the bus. One trip took us to Washington, DC, New York City, and Boston. In Washington, we were privileged to spend time with Richard Halverson, then

My cooking class

Chaplain of the Senate. He graciously answered probing questions for over an hour. For a few years, I took some students to Atlanta for the Palm Sunday weekend. The main attraction was always the Passion Play presented in the Civic Auditorium. It had started out small in a Baptist church, but within ten years it was being seen by sell-out crowds eight or nine times each year. To see and hear a quality production portraying Christ's life, death and resurrection was eye-opening in a whole new dimension for these students. The music was of professional quality. Bob and Lyn Culver are still hosting these special trips and arrange host families for the students to stay with in Atlanta.

Some of the students were interested in more in-depth Bible study and a class was started on Sunday morning to accommodate them.

On January 27, 1988, Rebekah Edith joined Shelley and Dieter's family. The last of the grandchildren, Camila Soules Neves, was born on August 16, 1988. Linda came from Brazil with both girls to spend Christmas in Chattanooga that year,

PART TWO: International Students, Inc.

joining Shelley's family for a very memorable occasion. In early January, '89, the Schmidts departed for Japan, and Linda took her girls to visit Baird's family and friends in Massachusetts.

In 1989, I was given permission from the Overseas Ministry Division of ISI to join a group from the 4 C's to attend a meeting in southern Brazil. The US Congregational denomination met with the World Evangelical Congregational Alliance. It was a wonderful experience. Quoting from a letter I wrote after that trip, "I was encouraged to see the strong Brazilian leadership which has developed since we left the field in 1974. The Brazilian churches, both the Presbyterian and the Congregational denominations, are now sending missionaries to Portugal and other Portuguese speaking countries. I was privileged to be a part of this second World Evangelical Congregational Fellowship. It was so interesting to hear about the efforts of numerous Evangelicals all over the world looking for a common bond, which was Christ."

Taking advantage of my being in Brazil, I flew north to Salvador to visit Linda and the family. Catarina was already 4 ½ and Camila was 13 months old and just starting to walk. Those first steps reminded me of how cautious and anxious we all are as we try something new. Only after many mistakes, and many falls, do we get the ability and confidence to step out "in faith."

Before I left Salvador, I had a visit from dear friends from our years in Crato. Iracy and a younger sister, Ilza, had taken a 12 hour bus trip to see me. What a joy to see them again.

Returning home, I soon got back into the routine of meeting with the students. I had been having a weekly Bible study with a girl from Japan. She had returned home and I endeavored to keep in contact with her, encouraging her in the faith. One student from Nigeria had been studying in Chattanooga for six years, and we had some good conversations. His financial situation was precarious, and he decided he would have to return home before obtaining his Master's degree. The last night before he left, I had a long talk with him, and the way of salvation became clear to him. The seed had been planted by conversation with the Assistant Pastor, and now his spiritual eyes were opened. He went home with a new life to share with his wife and three children. What a joy to see this renewal in a person's heart and mind.

Over the intervening years, men who have proved Him to be what He claims to be, have been forever changed by the UN-CHANGING ONE.

For several years, I accompanied some international students to the Florida Conference held from December 26th to January 2nd. We always did a lot of sight-seeing at Disney World and Epcot. On their evaluation forms turned in at the end, it consistently showed how much they appreciated their host families and the conversations on the bus going and coming. Some made decisions for Christ during these trips. Their knowledge of God's plan for their lives left an indelible impression which was helped to grow in the months to follow.

For a few years I was on the ACMI Board. This is an organization of "American Christians Ministering to Internationals." Some in our group at church accompanied me to ACMI Conferences where we were able to assimilate ideas and inspiration from others working with internationals and use the ideas in Chattanooga.

My days were full, and I loved it. I continued tutoring in 1990 and invited several of the students to dinner at Easter. Holidays proved to be good times to get together and go on picnics or to open our homes. Two years in a row, I took some students to the Thanksgiving Conference in Nashville. It was a thrill to have Michael Card participate in these conferences, thanks to his friendship with John Eaves. I continued to function as Registrar for the Regional Conference of ISI, which was at King College in June. However, I still had difficulty using my time wisely. Andrew Murray gave good advice, "Time is a quantity that accommodates itself to our will; what our hearts really consider of first importance in the day we will soon succeed

PART TWO: International Students, Inc.

Michael Card

in finding time for." It's easy to forget this crucial reminder.

ISI is a wonderful organization that appreciates the contributions from people of all ages. It is especially true that Asian students look up to those who are "older and wiser." It was decided, through conversations with the authorities in Colorado Springs, that I could be working fewer hours and downsize to Senior Status. Before this move, which would involve diminished finances, I got a new computer.

How thankful I am that I was able to keep up, in a limited capacity, with the computer age. It was and is such a help in my involvement with the students. My mail list was a little top-heavy, but I appreciated having so many friends from various locations with whom I was able to keep in contact. How thankful I am to God for directing our steps into ISI in 1984, when, from a worldly point of view, it seemed rather "foolhardy" to leave the pastorate five years before retirement age. Only the Lord knew when Frank's "retirement" was to take place, and how I would need a ministry I could participate in when we were no longer a "team." God has abundantly provided above all I could even ask or think.

I officially retired in 1994 from ISI. I was presented with a certificate for my 10 years with this ministry when I attended a conference in Colorado Springs. Being retired did not mean a noticeable reduction in contacts with my beloved students. Through the mail and e-mail I was able to "bridge the oceans" as students completed their studies and returned to their homelands. I feel my retirement was more of a "retread." Like putting a new surface on an old tire, so as to extend its usefulness, I hoped that by doing different things with the international students, my involvement could be extended.

I still enjoy meeting new students who come to our monthly activities. Just as I was becoming less involved, others were seeing the challenges and the opportunity to reach these students. We had our 6th Fall Picnic in 1995, and a bigger crowd of students and friends made it a success. We chose a name for this group of interested church people, and "First Friends" became an integral part of the ministry at First Presbyterian.

The summer of 1996 was significant when the Olympics took place within 100 miles of Chattanooga. Some of my thoughts about that event were in a letter sent out to those on my mail list. "The eyes of the world will be focused on all the events taking place just south of here. How different, yet how similar was the day of Pentecost when 'God-fearing Jews from every nation of the world,' were in Jerusalem. They had one purpose, but beyond that known purpose, God had another. Many hundreds will be bringing this ageless message to countless athletes in Atlanta. Let's be praying for that secondary purpose and the impact He will have on ready hearts."

In June 1998, ISI wanted to honor retirees and invited us to attend the annual conference as their guests. What a privilege to see many old friends who had faithfully served the Lord reaching out to internationals. Retirement has not kept us from further involvement with the students.

Travels

I have always loved to travel. It's a good thing, with my children in three continents and the conferences of ISI and the 4C's in many areas of the country.

I had a wonderful trip to Japan in the summer of '91. We went by van and ferry (18 hours) to Otaru on the island of Hakkaido. On the ferry we slept in bunks with curtains giving each one a little privacy. We visited the Language School in Sapporo and stayed two nights in the mission house on Lake Toya. Back in Tokyo, I contacted one of my former students and spent the day with her. Two of the wives who had been in my Cooking Classes met us in a large park with their families. It was great to see them again.

Sawako and Kimiko and their families meet the Schmidts and me in Tokyo.

Japan is a long way from Chattanooga, but I enjoyed the trip and finally got rested after returning home. That Christmas was spent with Baird and his family in Massachusetts. I was also able to speak in five of my supporting churches in Massachusetts, Connecticut and New York. In this way, they felt they had a "hands-on" connection with the ministry down South.

While in New York City on January 2, I missed a 2-inch step and broke the three bones in my elbow. That made a drastic change in plans. A four-hour operation and six days in the hospital was made only slightly more pleasant with visits from many friends I had known when we lived in the city. My colleague, Marion Paxton, was such a help and made frequent visits. When I was in Rehabilitation two days after surgery, my surgeon who was from Hong Kong came to see me. When I slightly moved my fingers which were poking out from the huge bandage, he remarked, "You must have had someone praying for you." I assured him I did, and I discovered he was a Christian who belonged to a Presbyterian church in Queens. He said that had I severed the nerve around those bones I probably would have lost the use of my hand. Six months later, my eleven-piece "erector set" was removed, and I was able to have full use of my hand, even though my left arm ended a bit shorter than the right one.

Using some accumulated Frequent Flier miles, I was able to visit Linda in Brazil in November, 1992. Before flying up North from Rio de Janeiro, I took the opportunity to visit a female doctor named Eusinia I had met through ISI in Atlanta. The two of us flew from Rio to Iguaçu to see the famous falls. There seems to be no end of them. One day we viewed them from the Brazil side, and the next day we took the bus to Argentina to see them from that vantage point. They are truly spectacular, and worth the extra effort to see them. (It's interesting to note the derivation of the word "cataract." In Portuguese, "catarata" means waterfall. It's really true that when one needs cataract surgery, it looks like one's vision is blurred as if looking through falling water.)

PART TWO: Travels

Dra. Eusinia at Iguaçu Falls

My friend had some doubts about Christianity, and I trust our talks and the book I gave her helped to lead her toward the Savior. I said goodbye to Eusinia and flew from Rio to Salvador which is about 800 miles north, with a much warmer climate. It was lovely to see the girls again. They had grown so much. One week the four of us took a bus to Recife to visit people we had worked with years before. The roads were so bad, and my back hurt so much, that we decided to fly home at the end of the week. After a lovely visit with Linda and my friends in Salvador, I was home in Chattanooga with just enough time to prepare for the Christmas celebrations and the party for the students. It was very special singing carols, making ornaments for the tree and having a wonderful meal.

In March of '93 I had an invitation to come to Hawaii. Chaplain Jerry Malone and his wife Judy had met Frank and me at the annual conferences of the 4C's. They were soon to leave their post in Hawaii and invited me to visit before they left. I was delighted to see them, and also to cross off my 49th state in my travels. The Imperial Palace was especially impressive. Joining others to see the USS Arizona Memorial was truly awe-inspiring as we remembered the hundreds of service men and women who were lost on that infamous day in 1941. The Malones were lovely hosts and showed me many other interesting places around the island. By visiting the tropical paradise of Hawaii that week, I missed the record snowstorm of '93, when 20 inches fell on Chattanooga in one day.

Frank's mom died in October, 1993, having lost her youngest son, Paul, only two weeks before. Fred, her oldest, survived her. Shelley and Dieter were spending their furlough in Massachusetts that year. Terrill arrived from Atlanta, and with Baird and Shelley, accompanied me at the funeral. She had lived a fruitful and blessed life for 97 years. She had faithfully prayed for her children, grandchildren and great-grandchildren. Quite a legacy!

Dale and Janet Tallman had been good friends for many years, and on December 27, 1993, they were married. I was only made aware of this after the fact, but I was happy for them.

I was talking with my good friend Therese Van Wickler one day saying I would love to visit Shelley in Switzerland where her family was spending some time before returning to Japan in 1994. Therese mentioned she would like to visit relatives in Germany, and from this evolved a month-long trip on the trains of Europe visiting some of the missionaries supported by our church. This itinerary was worked out by corresponding with those on the field. Some she knew, and some were known only by me. We found out shortly before our arrival in two of the homes that they had assumed "Therese and Ardy" were a couple, in as much as my name left gender up for grabs.

In May of '94, we purchased month-long Eurail passes and flew into Amsterdam, and on to Lisbon. As I was trying to be consistent about watching my weight, and Therese agreed, I ordered special meals on the flights. One was "Asian Vegetarian" and the other a "Low Cal meal." Dinner was palatable on the

PART TWO: Travels

flight to Holland, but the Asian Vegetarian breakfast left something to be desired – like breakfast. The flight to Lisbon was still in the morning hours, and so I got a repeat of my cucumber and pita bread sandwiches. I was so ready for some Portuguese bread and coffee when we arrived.

With Glenn and Frances Camenisch as our able hosts, we visited the oldest castle in Lisbon. The next day, they took us to Cascais and Estoril. In Sintra, we were enchanted by another old castle, with its many additions and colorful exterior. Our plans were to take the train to Madrid, but a Portuguese Rail strike altered those, so we flew in order to avoid missing our friends in this second capital city.

A castle in Sintra, Portugal

The Reeds and Krachts showed us many fascinating places in Madrid where they were reaching the Spaniards with the gospel. I loved Toledo, which is famous for pottery, enamel and gold jewelry. The Palace is no longer the residence for the King and Queen, but a few of the elegant rooms were open to visitors. I was getting a taste of the extravagance of royalty in Europe. A side trip to the Hacienda where the Kulls lived gave us another view of mission work in this country.

Our first use of the Eurail passes was from Madrid to Barcelona. We stayed in a hotel and toured the city the next day. We passed the venue for the Olympics of 1992 and also some very old Cathedrals and villages showing crafts of another era. My Portuguese was passable in Lisbon, but it didn't help much in Spain, even though the languages are so similar. Food choices were limited to what we could point to in a small café or read on a menu in English in a larger restaurant.

We boarded the train to take us to Nice, not realizing we were to change trains with a two-hour lay-over on the French border. It was 10 p.m. when we pulled into a grubby little station with no place to sit. Just before the exchange window closed, we obtained some Francs and bought something to eat. We ran into a couple of American guys from Georgia. They were tickled to meet someone from "back home." The amount of beer they were downing helped them feel "tickled" about everything. They offered to carry our bags down the stairs to the tracks, which was greatly appreciated. The picture of Therese carrying the can of Budweiser for one of the young men was a photo-op I hated to miss.

We parted company when we boarded the first class car. Those accommodations didn't mean much as we had no water in the rest rooms during the six hour trip to Nice. Linda and Joe Barnes met us in the morning and we were soon in Monte Carlo. They gave us a very interesting tour of the Trans World Radio Studio. Hitler had seen the station as a strategic location from which to broadcast his propaganda.

After the war ended, the purchase of this property facilitated sending forth propaganda of a different kind. It became a beacon of God's love to all who would hear. People from over 25 countries are working in this studio. As the programs come into the studio from several countries, they are edited and sent out so people can hear the good news in their own languages.

One amusing incident was when we were taken to see the beautiful lobby of the Casino in Monte Carlo. No one informed me I should hide my camera, and as I tried to photograph the interior, I was practically pounced on by security guards. Without some quick explanation in French by our hosts, assuring

PART TWO: Travels

Therese and Ardy in Monaco

the guards no pictures were taken, I might have lost my camera entirely. Not that I was seeking notoriety, but I know of none of my fiends who can claim they were forcefully escorted from the famous Casino.

From Nice, we boarded the train once more and were met in the huge station in Milan by John Verderame. There had been a border check going into Italy, with dogs sniffing for drugs. This delayed us for over an hour. Usually, the trains in Europe are on time to the minute. That evening, we enjoyed a nice meal and a family "concert." Catherine played the guitar and 3½ year old Robert sang along with her in English and Italian.

The next day's sight-seeing included the huge Duomo, the Galeria with its impressive glassed-in roof, and the Leonardo da Vinci Museum. In the section showing navigation around the world, they had a jangada, the Brazilian fishing raft so familiar to us in Brazil. I wanted to inform them the sail was situated on the raft incorrectly but, alas, the language barrier prevented it. These jangadas always had the point of the triangular sail embedded in the wooden raft, thus allowing the wind to catch a larger area.

Lugano, Switzerland, was our next stop, and we were still immersed in Italian, it being one of the four official languages of Switzerland. It was a delightful town and we toured by boat to see it from the water. From there, another train took us to Zurich through the most awesome mountain scenery of the whole trip. I was so enthralled by the beauty of the snow capped mountains and tiny "postcard-like" villages, I forgot to use my camera. We were now in the German-speaking section of Switzerland, and my Swiss son-in-law met us. One more train trip, all included in our Eurail Pass, took us to Wetzikon where my daughter and my three granddaughters met us with love and excitement.

The famous Galeria dome in Milan, Italy

After celebrating Mother's Day and Shelley and Dieter's birthdays in 1994, Therese left us to visit relatives in Germany, and I spent another week with the Schmidts. I was thrilled with our visit to the Garden Island of Mainau in Lake Constance. The flowers were gorgeous, and there was ample opportunity to capture their beauty on film.

As I said goodbye to Shelley and Dieter, it was sad to think I probably wouldn't see them for four years. (However, for Christmas, '95, Shelley was able to join her siblings for a lovely mini-reunion.) They were to return to Japan the next month. I

PART TWO: Travels

met Therese in Frankfurt. By then, her hip was really bothering her, and I realized my eyesight was deteriorating. We met our missionaries, the Stevens, in Geissen and then went to Heidelberg. Seeing these ancient cities makes one increasingly aware of the antiquity of buildings in Europe. Nothing is "old" until it's been around 400 years or more. It made me feel really young.

One of the students I had tutored at UTC four years before met us in Frankfurt. Christiane graciously took us around the city and also to the town of Mainz. From there we caught a boat on the Rhine. It was supposed to be a four-hour trip to Cologne, but being a holiday, they stopped at every little town on the way and extended our trip by five hours. It just gave us a longer time to view the many spectacular castles on the way to Cologne. Finding a hotel was not difficult, but sleeping was. The holiday crowd partied until 4:00 a.m. Before boarding our train for Amsterdam the next day, we made a brief stop at the very famous Cathedral in Cologne.

This completed our month's train adventure, and our hotel was close to the station. Therese didn't feel like venturing out to a restaurant because of her hip, so she suggested I go and bring back some familiar food from a McDonalds. It looked close enough on the map, so off I went. It turned out to be several blocks away, and not all that easy to find. But I came back with supper, happily, and I was very glad to be in for the night.

When we visited the Zider Zee Museum the next day, I was the "pusher" and Therese was the "pushee" in a wheelchair provided by the museum. This is a restored village giving us a picture of the country 100 years before. They showed us how they made wooden shoes, dainty handwork, jams and painted wooden articles. We would have liked to have visited the Ann Frank House and the "ten Boom House," but both were closed that day. We were delighted to take a canal tour which gave us a different perspective of the city. The month had gone swiftly by and we were once more checking in for our flight to Atlanta. My Asian Vegetarian menu came back to haunt me, as it was

Nayda and me, 1994

still listed under my name. Fortunately, enough regular meals were on board, so I was able to switch.

We had had a memorable trip. We were graciously treated by friends, old and new. We learned more about their work and also visited many historical places in each city. We had gotten a glimpse of seven countries in Europe which will always be etched in our memories. How thankful we were to arrive home safely. Unfortunately, Therese's hip did not improve and she needed surgery shortly after our return.

By the middle of July, 1994, I was off again, this time to the West Coast. My reason, primarily, was to attend our annual ISI Conference in Colorado Springs. I rationalized that if I was that far west, I might as well go to the coast first and see both sisters and my son and daughter-in-law. When in Washington State, we went out on my brother-in-law's yacht. They were exclaiming how beautiful Mt. Baker was that day. My left eye had rapidly gone from 20-20 to 20-400 in only a few months. So I said, "Point my camera to Baker so I can take a picture." Only after cataract surgery in August, 1994, was I able to see the photo

PART TWO: Travels

and remember the day when they were exclaiming how impressive the mountain was.

My first cruise was to Alaska in 1996. August was a great month for this and I really enjoyed it. I had a few hours in Anchorage and was amazed at the beautiful flowers in this city. With 18-20 hours of sunshine in the summer, the blossoms take on huge proportions. This cruise allowed me to complete visiting all 50 states.

Therese again went with me, but took a different flight out of Chattanooga. She was booked on two different flights, both of which were cancelled because of mechanical problems. When she finally arrived in Seattle, it was too late to reach Anchorage, where our cruise started. After missing two and a half days of the cruise, she finally boarded in Sitka.

The highlight for both of us was taking a helicopter ride from Juneau. We landed on the Mendenhall Glacier and for an hour we explored this frozen stretch of landscape on foot. The helicopter took us safely back to Juneau where we enjoyed the luxury of our ship. I was sorry that Therese had missed a great deal of the inspiring scenery of this northern state.

In November, 1996 I spent a few days with the Ewalds in New York City. One morning I walked the few blocks to a coffee shop on 72nd and Columbus. These are some of the observations I jotted down as I did some "people watching" and drank my coffee and ate a wonderful New York bagel. "People everywhere were walking their dogs. Runners with headphones were making their way to their offices and others were roller-blading to work. Pedestrians needed to be watchful as dozens of taxis turned left at corners with no thought of slowing down. Cars were double parked, and sometimes these were also double parked, while drivers ran in to get their first cup of coffee. There was a man in a Cadillac lighting his cigar as the light turned green and a taxi urged him to move out of his way. Bags and bags of trash were waiting to be picked up at that early hour. Couples were seen kissing goodbye and there were always poor people scrounging for what they could. All this happened between 7:40 and 8:20 and would be repeated on many corners and every day. One can get a feel for the people of this city in a short time, seeing ambitious drive, hopeless searching, and joyful enthusiasm in this microcosm of humanity. Most of them have not sensed their need for a Savior, but the need is universal, nevertheless."

In April, 1997, I was able to return to Switzerland once more to visit Shelley's family who were on a short furlough from their work in Japan. The beauty of that country never ceases to amaze me. I also love the ease of train travel over there. Shelley and I left the two girls with Dieter and did some sight-seeing in that beautiful country. We stayed overnight in Zermatt at the foot of the Matterhorn. We took a train the next day to get even closer to the base of the mountain, but it was covered in fog. We had only a couple of hours before we had to catch our train home, so we waited. We were awarded a glorious sight as the fog cleared and the famous peak came into view, giving us just enough time to get some wonderful photographs.

The Matterhorn viewed from Zermatt

When Dale and Janet moved to Pender Island in Canada, they invited me to join them for Thanksgiving. That is a beautiful part of North America. I enjoyed the many ferry trips while in Canada, but I would hate to plan EVERY trip around a ferry schedule.

Three years seemed to be as long as I could endure an interval between trips to Brazil. The spring of 1998 was spent in Salvador once more. Linda was doing a lot of teaching, so she was away a good bit during the day. I enjoyed being "pampered" by Linda's maid, and afternoon coffee was offered daily. I was able to read several books, and Linda and I often went to the Mall.

This was different from malls in the States. It was a "little city." The pharmacy, bank, post office and kiosks where they took one's blood pressure, all were present within its confines. Of course, many large stores and small specialty shops were generously spaced throughout, as well as the usual food court and Cinemas. Another difference from the states was the underground parking. One got a ticket upon entering the two or three floor garage and surrendered it when exiting. I misplaced this ticket once and we were delayed over half an hour as they checked our license plate and Linda's ID. I guess it's a good sys-

One of several parks in Salvador, Brazil

tem, and being able to park out of the sun is much appreciated. The big plus was being able to escape to an air conditioned environment and sit and chat over a cafezinho. Even though we had fans in her apartment, the heat was overwhelming at times.

Spending five or six weeks in another country helps me to become familiar once more with another culture. I enjoyed using my Portuguese each visit, but my vocabulary was suffering more and more as the years progressed. One time when I was with Linda and her family in February, Catarina, Linda and I celebrated our birthdays. We all had a good laugh when I suggested we put a blanket (cobertor) on the cake instead of frosting (cobertura.) It was easy for me to mix up these two words.

Driving is always a challenge in Salvador, but Linda was up to it. The hills rival those in San Francisco, and very few cars have automatic transmissions. She was very adept at the fancy "clutch" work required. Lack of air- conditioning means the windows are open to loud sounds, hot air, and little boys wanting to peddle something at each signal. As Linda was aware of certain corners where the boys were more aggressive, she would say "roll up the windows," until we were safely through the green light. When I returned to Chattanooga and began driving once more, I found I was often surpassing the speed limit. My windows were usually closed, and the speed I was driving was not apparent, as it was so much quieter. I had to keep my eyes on the speedometer for a while until I was used to being back home.

In December, 1998, it was special to have most of the children home for Christmas. Dale couldn't make it, but the others were with me, and we crowded out the condo, with the overflow spending their nights at a neighbor's house. In Atlanta, Catarina and Camila posed for a "Coke ad" at "The World of Coke."

In November, 1999, I made an unexpected trip to Japan. I just felt that I was needed as a Mom to give Shelley some encouragement at that time. I was only there for a short time, but

PART TWO: Travels

spent Thanksgiving with them and was able to see the Senior play, which was "The Christmas Carol." Andrea sang in it even though she wasn't a senior.

Two days after I arrived, Shelley and I took three trains into Tokyo and accepted the invitation to the Swiss Ambassador's residence. The Ambassador's wife gave a lovely tea and spent about fifteen minutes just talking with Shelley and me. She had been born in Kobe but had lived all over the world. We stopped at a mall on the way home. We had some coffee in cans from a vending machine. One could have it either hot or cold from the same machine.

Catarina and Camila modeling in a Coke ad

Dieter and the girls usually rode their bikes to school, with their lunches, their backpacks, and instruments (on Dieter's bike). They always had to leave really early. I had given Andrea Frank's trumpet in 1993 when she showed a real desire to learn this instrument. She has continued over the years and occasionally plays in the jazz band where she teaches.

One must follow some inner leading at times without completely understanding why. Shelley and I were both thankful I had made the effort to be there with them.

191

I returned to New York City in May, 2001 to visit my dear friends, the Ewalds. I had occasion to take a Circle Tour around Manhattan when I was able to capture this historical photo showing Trinity Church between the towers of the World Trade Center. Each of us will remember that horrendous day in September. It changed the lives of millions of people – how they felt and how they reacted. We are feeling the results to this day. It is significant that the church in the photo still stands as a sentinel in that strategic city.

Trinity Church seen between the twin towers of The World Trade Center

In June, 2002, Therese and I took another memorable trip. This time it was a cruise from Dover, England to the Scandinavian capitals. It was only my second cruise, and I love this mode of travel.

Getting to Dover, however, was somewhat of an adventure. We flew out of Boston to get bargain fares, but a huge thunderstorm that day delayed arriving planes from London. They were diverted to Maine, and so our bags, which had been checked hours before, were left outside to the mercy of the elements. In all, we spent a total of 12 hours in Logan Airport. When we eventually arrived in London, we discovered damp and drippy clothes in our luggage. The Grand Circle people were very accommodating, and insurance covered the cost of the clothes which had been damaged. It was quite a sight to see most of our clothes draped around every available space in our hotel room.

We spent two days seeing London before boarding our Norwegian Cruise Line ship in Dover. At Madam Tussaud's Wax Museum, we got "up close and personal" with many famous personalities. I even had my photo taken with Queen Elizabeth. From Dover, we left the North Sea for the Baltic by going through the Brunsbuttel Locks in the Kiel Canal. This was built in 1784 and enlarged in 1907. Before entering the Canal, the smokestack had to be lowered. This was called "Flipping of the Funnel" and our ship was the only one in the Norwegian fleet with this capability. It was interesting to see this huge hinged smokestack put down on its side. This was necessary because of the 9 bridges we went under, the minimum height being only 138 feet. The total passage through the Canal took ten hours.

Our first port of call was in Tallinn, Estonia. I loved walking around this quaint village. The Gothic Town Hall dates from 1371 and is the only surviving example of this type of architecture in the North. Our next stop was St. Petersburg in Russia. They scheduled two days, but it wasn't nearly enough. We arrived on July 4th, and in our honor we were greeted by a Russian band playing the *Star Spangled Banner.* St. Petersburg is a bustling city of 5 million people. It is "criss-crossed" with dozens of miles of waterways requiring 17 main bridges. When we arrived, the city was preparing for their 300th anniversary in 2003, so many of the buildings were camouflaged by scaffolding. The famous Hermitage Museum was incredibly beautiful, and our three-hour tour was like tasting a tiny bit of frosting of a wedding cake, expecting to experience the honeymoon. But what we did see was fascinating, with famous art work and sculptures throughout the buildings we entered. It's amazing that the country of Russia covers one sixth of the land surface of our globe and goes through 11 of the world's 24 time zones. Its shores are washed by twelve seas.

Navigating at night allowed us to greet the dawn in Helsinki, Finland. After Reykjavik in Iceland, Helsinki is the most northerly capital in Europe. There is a park commemorating the life of the famous composer, Jan Sibelius. We also visited the location of the Stadium where the Olympics were held in the summer of 1962.

Unfortunately, we only had a few hours each day in these Scandinavian capitals. Our next port of call was Stockholm, Sweden. They provided a wonderful tour of the City Hall where a banquet is held after awarding the Nobel prizes in another building. Alfred Nobel, for whom the prize is named, was born in Stockholm in 1833. He made his fortune from his discovery of dynamite, but wanted to set up these prizes to commemorate peace, education and science.

As we slowly made our way into the port at Copenhagen, Denmark, we were astounded by an enormous windmill farm at the shore line. Denmark is one of the world's leaders in alternative energy such as solar and windmill technology. One of the ship-arranged tours in Copenhagen was to the Tivoli Gardens. It was planned for us to stay after dark which gave us an extended opportunity to enjoy the huge lighted park. The Tivoli was built in 1843 by a Danish architect, and Walt Disney got his inspiration for Disneyland when he visited the park in the 20th century. There was entertainment in many areas, as well as numerous rides. Of course, a boundless variety of food was readily available.

Our last city on this memorable cruise was Oslo, Norway. There are many museums in Oslo, one showing the FRAM which Amundsen took to the South Pole. We were privileged to see the RaII, which was constructed entirely of reeds in 1970. The famous Kontiki constructed of balsa wood in 1947 was also on display. The 700-year-old fort along the dock emphasized once more the antiquity of the buildings and the need for protection in by-gone centuries.

Back in Dover, we boarded a bus once more, this time taking the "scenic route" and stopping at Windsor Castle. We

Part Two: Travels

were delighted to witness the impressive changing of the guard. "Fish and Chips" were definitely a must as we ate in a small pub before returning to London. As we flew home to Chattanooga, via Boston, we both agreed that this cruise had been an unforgettable experience.

Later that summer approximately 300 of us gathered in North Carolina for a Brazil Reunion. There were former Brazil missionaries, ones presently ministering in Brazil, and many children and grandchildren of those present. We ranged in age from two months to 94 years. What a great time to renew friendships, sing in Portuguese and *"matar saudades"* (literally to kill homesickness), after thirty years.

As has become common to so many families, two of my children have been divorced. Terrill, divorced in 1988, has since gotten happily remarried to Foster Bolton, mother of Addie and Clay. Linda got a divorce in 1999 and still lives in Salvador with her two daughters.

I made another trip west in September, 2003, visiting both Dale and Janet and my sister Nayda and her husband Beecher in Seattle. I am so thankful I am able to keep going to visit my "far-flung" family. I was particularly impressed with the glass museum in Tacoma, Washington. The work of the glass blower extraordinaire, Dale Chihuly, a native of Tacoma, was incredible. Two years after this visit, I was in Atlanta with Terrill and Foster. Several of Chihuly's glass exhibits complementing the various plants and flowers were in The Botanical Gardens. It was impossible to capture their beauty on film, but many of us tried, nevertheless.

In June, 2004, I returned to Massachusetts; this time for my granddaughter's wedding to Ben Greene. Jessica had chosen the date of June 20, which carried on this tradition to the 3rd generation. It was such a lovely outdoor wedding with the reception under a huge tent with hanging baskets of flowers decorating the whole place. Shelley was in Massachusetts for a short time so she and I were able to attend, as were Terrill and

Athena. We were all so thankful for beautiful weather so we could really enjoy being outdoors. It had rained several days in the preceding two weeks.

Shelley and Dieter spent the holidays, 2004, in Switzerland with his family. Hannah was studying in Germany and Andrea

Josafa's son Josadoc with his wife Laceni and Linda

Cilas Cunha and Tontonha, Ardy, Laceni and Josadoc

had been doing student teaching in Basel. Many years had gone by since they had been with Dieter's parents for Christmas.

I read once that seniors are in one of three groups: the "go-go's," the "slow-go's" and the "no-go's." Group two is creeping up on me, but I want to avoid group three if at all possible.

Using frequent flier miles or getting good fares allowed me to make additional trips to Brazil in 2000, 2003 and 2005. My last trip to Brazil was in the summer of 2005. Linda, the girls and I flew from Salvador to Recife and were graciously hosted by Cilas Cunha and Tontonha. It was a blessing to see them again. They had been active in the Lord's work with Frank more than 20 years before. Cilas is tremendously busy running three schools which prepare students for the university. Josadoc and Laceni were also living in Recife. He is the son of Josafá, the evangelist who helped Frank so much in Crato.

We also had a short visit with Flávio. Frank had helped him come to Massachusetts to study music many years before and he was presently using his musical talent directing many choirs. He always loved to accompany Frank on the piano and spoke of all that Frank's friendship had meant to him.

As I reviewed these friendships in person, it was very meaningful to me. Catarina was studying Chemical Engineering in the University, and Camila was going to be in college by the next year. Keeping up with their progress with my visits south and their visits north helped me to feel close to the grandchildren. It was always great to have extended time with Linda, of course. All three had come to spend Christmas with me in 2004, the first time since 1998.

Shortly after I returned from Brazil, my older sister lost her battle with recurring illnesses and passed away in September.

In March, 2006, I visited Nayda and Beecher in Palm Desert, California, for two weeks. They escape some Seattle dampness during the winter. I was delighted to have this time with them. We had a very special reunion with my two cousins, Ruth

The Denmans, Nayda and Beecher

Denny Denman, Jack and Lyn Walls, and Ruth Denman

Champion Denman and Lyn Davis Walls (and their husbands) who had been my bridesmaids 60 years before. Nayda was the other bridesmaid, so only my sister Janet was missing.

PART TWO: Travels

I boarded the Coast Starlight in Los Angeles and had a marvelous train trip to Seattle. In the course of thirty-five hours one passes by long stretches of the Pacific Ocean, the fertile valleys, dense forests and snow-covered mountains. Mount Hood looms high with its perpetual white cap shining before we approach Seattle. Dale and Janet met me in pouring rain, but it was nice to have a few days visiting them in their new home in Port Orchard. Of all the train trips I have taken, this is my favorite.

In all my travels, I've had some bags delayed, but never lost. It takes me longer to recuperate from a trip, but I guess that is to be expected. I hope I can enjoy good enough health to keep on visiting friends and family in the future.

Medical Interludes

For the most part, my health has been fairly stable for the last twenty years, but there have been a few "bumps" in the road. I've already mentioned my broken elbow which slowed me down somewhat in 1992.

Sometimes, it is the medical condition of one of the students that is cause for concern. In one of the papers I was correcting for a student from Taiwan, he mentioned he had a form of Muscular Dystrophy. Through the help of another student, I was able to direct T. to the Siskin Foundation here in Chattanooga. They were able to help him and he was extremely thankful. He put a Christian witness in every paper he wrote.

My granddaughter, Jessica, contracted Lyme Disease when she was seven, in 1992, during the time they were camping on Cape Cod. After some months of treatment, she was left with only minor effects of the disease, for which we are truly grateful.

It was in 1994 that my eyesight was deteriorating. Those little green arrows indicating a "left turn" were no longer visible. My cataract surgery was still two weeks away, but I decided to quit driving until afterwards. Definitely a good idea! Both eyes were operated on within a month, with no complications, thankfully. It was such a relief to be able to read and drive once more.

The Bible instructs us to walk by "faith and not by sight." Well, the "sight" was taken care of, but that didn't eliminate the "faith" part of it. The next crisis I faced was the "walking" part of the equation. My right knee gave out, and I needed a knee replacement in October, 2000. The doctors were correct in assessing what was needed, and after a couple months of rehabilitation, I was walking without any pain for a change. I had started taking Juice Plus+® two years prior to this. This is a nutritional product which gives one whole fruits and vegetables in capsule form. The rehabilitation nurses were impressed with my quick recovery and early mobility. I think all that good nutrition helped me recover more quickly. Of course, the prescribed exercises had to be continued faithfully, which also helped my recuperation.

Before this surgery was scheduled, I had planned to join a tour going to the Rose Parade on New Year's Day, 2001. I certainly didn't want to miss this chance to visit Pasadena, my hometown, and see my beloved parade in person. We kept our reservations and Therese went with me. At that point, the pain was still with me, but with the use of a cane, I even made it to our reserved seats on those high bleachers. It was a thrill to be there. In conjunction with the tour, we spent one day in the huge tents preparing flowers for the floats. We wore sweat shirts provided by the Lutheran Church with the title "Petal Pushers" on the front. It's incredible the number of hours put in by thousands of volunteers, in order to prepare for this parade, unequalled in beauty and technological elements. As a young girl, I loved going early on the parade day, when Dad was one of the official photographers.

Another highlight of being in Pasadena was when Therese and I hired a taxi for a couple of hours and revisited special places I remembered. We went by my home where I spent most of my childhood, the hospital where I was born, Pasadena City College, where I attended, and Fuller Seminary where Frank had graduated in 1954. It was a nostalgic time and the week was truly memorable.

In February, 2001 my mammogram showed a possible malignancy. A biopsy proved this to be true and surgery for a lumpectomy was scheduled. I was thankful this was caught early. They followed the operation with six and a half weeks of radiation as a further precaution. I have passed the five year mark now with no more treatment needed or relapse, which is cause for thanksgiving.

Part Two: Medical Interludes

My home on Navarro St. in Pasadena, California

In December, 1998, my granddaughter, Athena, had surgery for a brain tumor. Although it was not malignant, she has needed an additional surgery since then, and still suffers from occasional seizures. She has experienced much improvement over the years and can lead a normal life. I am so thankful for her and her sweet attitude through all this difficult time. Spending her college years in New York, she graduated from the Pratt Institute of Design in 2001. She has gladly agreed to do the art work for the cover of this book.

On June 11, 2002, Nathaniel's son Alixander made me a great-grandmother. He suffered a medical crisis from the day he was born, and needed open heart surgery when he was a week old. They needed to transpose the arteries from the lungs and the heart. This was done successfully and today, at five years old, he is a healthy, active little boy.

Shelley suffered a traumatic accident in 2005 when a van hit her

Alix at one year

while she was riding her bike in Japan. Although she suffered much facial injury and a broken wrist, we are so thankful for her surviving this accident with no permanent disability.

Family Reunion 2006

As in the case of the reunion in 1986, the planning had been in progress for over a year. This time schedules had to coordinate, not with babies and toddlers, but with college and career grandchildren. With the exception of Andrea, who was teaching near Atlanta, the rest of Shelley's family arrived from Japan. It was the beginning of their year's Home Assignment, and they rented a house nearby. Linda and the girls came from Brazil and extended their stay three more weeks after the reunion. Dale and Janet were living out west in the Seattle area. Baird and Carol, their two children and Jessica's husband flew from Massachusetts where they worked or studied. Terrill and Foster were both teaching in Atlanta, but their children came

Together again: Randall, Shelley, Baird, Linda, Dale and Terrill

All my grandchildren: Jason and his wife, Erin, Athena, Nathaniel, Andrea, Hudson, Jessica and Ben Greene, Catarina, Hannah, Aaron, Rebekah and Camila.

from New York City, San Francisco, and one studying in Atlanta. Foster's son was working in Spain and was unable to be with us. Randall and Ginny lived here in the city. He certainly did the "lion's share" of planning for this momentous event. Their oldest was married and lived in Knoxville, and one son lived here in Chattanooga. I figured that the combined miles covered by the 25 of us were well over 100,000. Rather amazing, to say the least.

When we all gathered at a local hotel to help me celebrate my 80th birthday, it was a very emotional time. A few of the grandchildren had not seen each other for twenty years. Including the two spouses, there were fourteen grandchildren in all, and often they would go out as a group and had hilarious experiences. Sometimes it was teaching a new dance in the lobby after midnight, or having cake and ice cream at a coffee shop down the street.

My boys had brought a variety of audio visual equipment which enabled us to see slides and videos of our previous get-

PART TWO: Family Reunion 2006

Our family reunion, 2006, in Chattanooga, Tennessee: From left, front row, Jessica, Andrea, Hannah, Rebekah, Catarina, Ardy, Erin, Janet and Ginny; 2nd row, Ben Greene, Shelley, Dieter, Aaron, Athena, Carol, Camila, Linda and Randall; top row, Hudson, Dale, Jason, Terrill, Nathaniel and Baird. Not in photo: Foster Soules, Addie and Clay.

together. Shelley's family got in on the fun by presenting a skit videoed in Japan of Dieter and Rebekah as clowns with unusual musical ability.

In the evening, the manager of the Staybridge Suites kindly gave us permission to use the tables in the lobby. One night, many made Be-De cards showing collages and sayings significant to the occasion. These were 4 x 6 index cards that Baird had initiated the year before. He always had cards, pencils, scissors and tape with him to record any event he was involved in at the time. These were shown as slides another evening.

The last day of the reunion, we gathered at Randall and Ginny's house taking advantage of many photo opportunities. After a delicious meal, they surprised me with a decorated birthday cake. A large card with sentiments written by each one was presented to me. This was definitely a surprise, being five months after the fact.

A very emotional time followed when each of us shared something about ourselves – in 90 seconds each. Some took longer, but it was an amazing and meaningful time of coming together in a spirit of love and harmony – especially for those who had not been a part of the family before. There was joy, laughter and tears with an overflowing of thankfulness for this special family. My prayer is that in the future we will all be included in God's family as a result of believing in Jesus Christ. Terrill recorded that evening so we all can relive it in the future.

I really don't mind being this age. Douglas MacArthur said it well at the end of World War II, "In the central place of every heart there is a recording chamber. So long as it receives messages of beauty, hope, cheer and courage, so long are we young. When the wires are all down and your heart is covered with snows of pessimism and cynicism, then and only then are you growing old." I trust the Lord will keep me looking to Him always with a positive attitude. Someone has said, "Better than counting your years, is making all your years count."

The next morning was "check-out" time and we separated to our far-flung locations. Actually, Linda's family delayed their return, and Shelley and Dieter had rented a house, so it was nice to have more extended time with all of them. Before leaving, each one had written their special memories in a "guest book" which I will always treasure. We felt we all had been privileged to be together, and we certainly knew and loved each other more deeply when it was over.

In any biographical history, there has to be a stopping point – either by death or a logical end to the story. I have no idea how many years I have left, but I can trust the One who does. This adventure of putting my life down on paper has been an enriching experience and one I trust will add some insight and humor to the lives of each one who reads it. May it be evident that God has led and is still leading in my life. I am still very much a Christian under construction. I can certainly agree with the author, Gert Behanna: "Lord, I'm not what I ought to be; I'm not what I'd like to be; I'm not what I'm going to be, but thank God, I'm not what I used to be."

Although some decisions did not seem to make sense at the time, yet, in hindsight, it was evident that God was giving unfailing guidance. For this I am truly grateful. May you feel blessed as you have shared in my life and look forward to creating many wonderful memories of your own.

"Do not count your years,
but make your years count."

An After-Christmas Poem

Christmas has come and gone for yet another year
For most it was merry, a time of good cheer.
A time for gathering with friends far away
And families stop over for a week or a day.

> We love to give gifts and it's nice to receive
> People have jammed each shop and each store,
> Even after the Day, they'll be crowded once more,
> And many will say, "It's over, I'm relieved".

How did this start, do we remember the reason?
If asked, could we give the "why" for this season?
A baby was born two millennia ago
No TV announcements, no photos to show.
But of such importance, there shown a bright star
And shepherds and wise men came from afar.
The story; repeated for each generation
This babe would be King and receive adoration.

Angels had come to tell Mary, the mother
Her babe would be born, unlike any other.
It's recorded in the Bible, God's Holy Word
But many today find the story absurd.

Soon the New Year will start and it will be '07
This Babe we call JESUS can lead us to Heaven.
His gift to us is for all who believe,
Like all Christmas gifts, it's ours to receive.

Ardy Soules 2006

~~TO ORDER~~
Heritage of Faithfulness
A Legacy of Love

Please send information below with check or money order to
Ardys Soules, 3701 Cherryton Drive, #12 , Chattanooga, TN 37411.
OR
Order online at www.waldenhouse.com
Waldenhouse Publishers, Inc., 100 Clegg St., Signal Mt, TN 37377

Name _____

Address: _____

_____

City _____ State _____ Zip _____

Telephone: _____

E-mail address (optional) _____

Ship to address if different: _____

_____

City _____ State _____ Zip _____

_____ (quantity) @ $14.95 US   = $ _____

Shipping 1st book (USA only) $4.60   = $ _____
For international rates and carriers, please contact the author.

Ship each additional book $3.00   = $ _____

Tennessee residents add sales tax @ 9.25%   = $ _____

                TOTAL   = $ _____

Mail with check or money order to:
Ardys Soules, 3701 Cherryton Drive, #12, Chattanooga, TN 37411
ardysoules@bellsouth.net
OR
Order online at www.waldenhouse.com
Waldenhouse Publishers, Inc., 100 Clegg St., Signal Mt, TN 37377

Warnock Pro on LSI 50# white
Type and design by Karen Stone